PLANE

ON
HUMAN AFFAIRS

Books on Astrology by Dr. B. V. Raman

Astrology for Beginners
A Manual of Hindu Astrology
A Catechism of Astrology
Hindu Predictive Astrology
How to Judge a Horoscope Vol. I
How to Judge a Horoscope Vol. II
Three Hundred Important Combinations
Prasna Marga Vol. I
Prasna Marga Vol. II
Prasna Tantra
Notable Horoscopes
My Experiments with Astrology
Nirayana Tables of Houses
Bhavartha Ratnakara
Ashtakavarga System of Prediction
Graha and Bhava Balas
Hindu Astrology and the West
Planetary Influences on Human Affairs
Muhurta or Electional Astrology
Studies in Jaimini Astrology
Klachakra Dasa
Raman's One Hundred Ten Years Ephemeris (1891-2000)

PLANETARY INFLUENCES ON HUMAN AFFAIRS

(Revised and enlarged edition of the book previously published as 'Astrology and Modern Thought')

BANGALORE VENKATA RAMAN

Editor : THE ASTROLOGICAL MAGAZINE

UBSPD

UBS Publishers' Distributors Pvt. Ltd.

New Delhi • Bangalore • Kolkata • Chennai • Patna • Bhopal
Ernakulam • Mumbai • Lucknow • Pune • Hyderabad

UBS PUBLISHERS' DISTRIBUTORS PVT. LTD.

5 Ansari Road, **New Delhi**-110 002
Phones: 011-23273601-4, 23266645-47

10 First Main Road, Gandhi Nagar, **Bangalore**-560 009
Phones: 080-22253903, 22263901, 22263902, 22255153

8/1-B Chowringhee Lane, **Kolkata**-700 016
Phones: 033-22521821, 22522910, 22529473

60 Nelson Manickam Road, Aminjikarai, **Chennai**-600 029
Phones: 044-23746222, 23746351-2

Ground Floor, Western Side, Annaporna Complex, 202 Naya Tola,
Patna-800 004 • Phones: 0612-2672856, 2673973, 2686170

Z-18, M.P. Nagar, Zone-I, **Bhopal**-462 011
Phones: 0755-4203183, 4203193, 2555228

No. 40/7940-41, Kollemparambil Chambers, Convent Road,
Ernakulam-682 035 • Phones: 0484-2353901, 2363905

2nd Floor, Apeejay Chambers, 5 Wallace Street, Fort,
Mumbai-400 001 • Phones: 022-66376922, 66376923, 56028017

1st Floor, Halwasiya Court Annexe, 11MG Marg, Hazaratganj,
Lucknow-226 001 • Phones: 0522-2294134, 2611128

680 Budhwar Peth, 2nd floor, Near Appa Balwant Chowk,
Pune-411 002 • Phone: 020-66028921

NVK Towers, 2nd floor, 3-6-272/B, Himayat Nagar,
Hyderabad-500 029 • Phones: 040-23262572, 23262573, 23262574

Visit us at www.ubspd.com & www.gobookshopping.com

Twelfth Edition	1992	Fifth Reprint	1998
First Reprint	1993	Sixth Reprint	2001
Second Reprint	1994	Seventh Reprint	2004
Third Reprint	1994	Eight Reprint	2006
Fourth Reprint	1996		

Printed at: Ram Printograph, Delhi

CONTENTS

PREFACE TO FIRST EDITION

In this book I have tried to present a case for astrology, and to refute the charge that a belief in astrology implies a belief in fatalism which in its turn paralyses human endeavour and retards human progress. Fate and Freewill are relative terms. Science cannot leave things in nature to blind chance and so-called necessity.

There is a good deal of misunderstanding and wrong notions about astrology, Karma etc., due partly to ignorance, partly to indifference and mainly to preconceived opinions.

The philosophy of astrology has as its strongest weapon relativity, and is based on the truth that ethereal vibrations extend from the Sun to the great planets and from planet to planet. All space is a network of interacting forces.

I have tried to prove that the concept of Karma Theory is not a wishful imagination but a product of daring thinking based upon cause-effect relationship so clearly discernible in physical phenomena. Bertrand Russell, Jung, Plank, Heisenberg, Bohr and Eddington have all been quoted to show that Modern Thought has been approaching the fringe of Reality realised by the Maharshis of India thousands of years ago. In fact, I have tried to link up traditional philosophy with modern scientific thought. The new concepts about space, time, matter and the universe have after all revealed that astrology marks the relationship between man's conscious ego and what we call Nature.

No 'scientific authority' accepts the suggestion that the proper way of dealing with the problems of astrology is not to theorise about and condemn them but to investigate them by the aid of well-attested facts. Such an idea seems to be quite foreign to the habits of thought of our scientific opponents. As Dr. Richard Garnette wrote, "the study of facts and the observation of nature must always be stronger than any abstract reasoning; and the investigation of the arguments brought against astrology will disclose a great reluctance on the part of the objector to resort to the testimony of facts, and a thoroughly unscientific habit of mind."

If I have succeeded in stimulating modern thinkers to take a more positive interest in the investigation of astrological truths, my labours will have been amply rewarded.

Bangalore
5-12-1946

B. V. RAMAN

PREFACE TO TWELFTH EDITION

PLANETARY INFLUENCES ON HUMAN AFFAIRS incorporates material based on investigations into cosmic-terrestrial relations that are being carried on by several men of science with whom I had the good fortune of personal discussion during my visits to Europe and America.

Chapters dealing with the relation of Astrology to medicine, weather forecasting, and predicting earthquakes have been added. The last chapter "Astrology vs Futurology" adopts a challenging tone questioning the scare-mongering forecasts of the "Futurologists" and assuring the public, on the basis of ancient Hindu astronomical and astrological concepts, that the world will not be destroyed for millions of years to come.

Experimental evidence presented in these pages cannot fail to impress even those orthodox scientists who continue to believe that a branch of knowledge to be valid should fit into the framework of known laws of science, and not otherwise.

Scientific laws which our text-books have taught us to look upon as eternal truths have collapsed like a pack of cards and new ones still lack the authority that their predecessors enjoyed. Scientists have also grown a little more circumspect and no longer proclaim general laws with the facility of their 19th century predecessors. Because of these developments, some of the scientists in the West have begun to view Astrology with less scepticism and more seriousness.

In Carl Jung's opinion, "Western civilisation, by ignoring Astrology, gains little and may be losing much" by what he calls "the contemptible treatment and defamation of an ancient art which defied a reasonable explanation" and, "after 200 years of intensive scientific progress, we can risk testing them in the light of modern truths."

This book explores certain concepts cherished by generations of thinkers in India that vicissitudes taking place in any part of the heavens must have their repercussions on human affairs because man is a part and parcel of the universe.

Thanks are due to UBS Publishers' Distributors Ltd., New Delhi, for having brought out this new edition attractively.

Dr. B.V. Raman

"Sri Rajeswari"
Bangalore-560 020
1st February, 1992

I

INTRODUCTORY

It has been customary to assert that until the coming of modern science, man was loaded down with superstition. It is far too easy for some of the so-called educated persons to dismiss certain fields of knowledge as astrology as unscientific because of ignorance. Astrology has been revealing, and this is amply borne out by researches of scientists in the West, a set of rational hypothesis challenging some of the orthodox scientific beliefs with their materialistic and deterministic tenets.

How did the astrological laws come into being ? Upon what kind of postulates were they based ? Was astrology an obstacle to progress or was it the reverse ? These questions can only be answered by a meticulous analysis of the philosophy of the complex culture which fashioned the thinking of the sages who brought astrology into being with the other branches of knowledge. The sages viewed astrology as a quest for verifiable knowledge. They were not primitive men merely conscious of the lure of the heavenly bodies as some of the modern educated ignoramuses think. The greatest superstition of today is the thinking that until the age of Galileo or Newton, man was ignorant. This fictitious belief has been systematically spun by a section of the Western thinkers and assiduously contrived by some of their Indian counterparts. Before Darwin, there was a Kanada in India; before Newton, there was a Bhaskara; and before any other physicist or biologist worth his name came on the scene, there were sages like Parasara and scientists like Varahamihira who were creative innovators and who recognised the simple but profound truth that man and the universe were not unrelated. The strivings of these sages are our heritage and they found the way by means of which we can unlock the door of Time.

In India, astrology had always occupied a unique place and found illustrious supporters until perhaps the advent and consolidation of the British power when for a time scepticism and derision were the predominant features, characterising the intellectual equipment of the then educated Indians, who looked down upon astrology and allied subjects as fit for study only by unscientific minds. In fact, the downfall of astrology appeared irremediable. It was at this time that late Prof. B. Suryanarain Rao undertook the task of reviving the subject by diverting the thoughts of the Indian cultured public to the secrets of a unique class of phenomenon, hitherto the object of ridicule to others who pass for better minds under the convenient name of men of science. For a time the mere use of the word astrology was likely to create an attitude of disparagement which effectually prevented many people from an impartial examination of the facts.

Today a great desire for serious study of astrology has overtaken the vast majority of the educated people.

Even today the attitude of some of the educated people here and in the West is still largely dominated by nineteenth century materialism which is generally unsympathetic not only to claims of astrology but to the spiritual view of life in general.

But Indian society has been permeated by faith in the spiritual aspect of things and fortunately today a great desire for serious study of astrology has overtaken the majority of the educated people.

There is great grass roots to support for a radical and thorough reinvestigation of the general standpoint of Astrology as a branch of science of permanent interest, capable of adding to the sum-total of human knowledge. There is keen desire that the contributions to culture and civilisation made by our Maharshis (sages) in the past should be brought to light today when India has achieved national independence and resumed her free career as a civilised self-governing nation in the van of advanced nation of the world.

The general scepticism consequent on the prevalent materialism derived passively from western currents of thought should not come in the way of the claims of astrology being recognised as a contribution to modern science and the art of life in general, especially for the reason that such sceptical attitudes are being counteracted by many powerful trends even in the West. The latest advances in relativity and atomic physics have led to second thoughts even amongst men of science themselves. Einstein himself has expressed in favour of theistic hypothesis. Eddington and Jeans have been led from the intelligibility of astronomical phenomena in the remotest galaxies to the idea of a Cosmic Intelligence indwelling in them in some mysterious way.

The materialists and sceptics have never had their own way at any time whether in the East or the West. In India we had the Lokayats or Charvakas (pure materialists) but they were few and far between and they could not maintain their position against the dominant schools.

In view of the vast mass of evidence in support of astrology, the attitude of deriders would appear to be the very reverse of scienttfic. In fact, as Dr. Whitehead has pointed out, modern materialism is not a straight reading from science at all but a misreading in terms of prejudice misled by the popular idea of sticks and stones—unthinking substances unrelated to consciousness.

Dr. Whitehead has put it on record that modern scientists have their own superstitions. This is valuable testimony, coming as it does from such a great mathematician.

It may be said that in the eyes of commonsense, there is an antecedent improbability or even impossibility in the claims of astrology the essence of which is that the planets and stars in their positions and mutual relations influence human lives in their minute particulars.

This antecedent impossibility will be seen in its true proportion when we realise that even the simplest act of the interaction of mind and matter, will and the nervous system in our own bodies, has yet been unexplained in terms of materialism. There is an antecedent impossibility of their interaction, on the commonsense hypothesis of their utter desperateness —or even on the refined hypothesis of Descartes of the dualism of mind and matter as utterly different substances.

The world, as a matter of fact, is so full of mystery that commonsense materialism can make nothing of it. To use Shakespeare's language, there are more things in Heaven and Earth than are dreamt of in Horatio's Philosophy.

Astrology has a long history from the dawn of civilisation. In India we have evidence of astrological knowledge even in the great classics, the Ramayana and the Mahabharata.

It is on record that Hindu astrologers at Alexander's Court predicted his death by poisoning in Babylon. Alexander avoided that city for a time but in the end, he entered it and died as foretold. Julius Ceasar consulted astrology in his battle dispositions and was successful but could not pay heed to the warning of Spurina that he would die on the Ides of March. Napoleon, it is well known, was advised by the famous woman astrologer Lenormand who repeatedly advised him not to march on Moscow but he disregarded her warning and met his fate. In medieval Europe, of course, astrology occupied an honoured place. Albertus Magnus, regarded as the father of scientific method, though a schoolman and theologian thought that wise men could annul or modify the effect of stars. Lord Bacon, the father of modern scientific method (The Advancement of Learning) was himself a competent astrologer. He saw no contradictions between science and astrology. He held that astrology should "rather be purged than rejected".

Even the great Newton, the formulator of the Laws of Motion supposed to be the cornerstones of materialism, able to banish God from the universe, was himself an astrologer. He had a collection of astrological works in his library and when his friend and pupil Halley protested to him about his regard for astrology, he replied: "I have studied these things and you have not."

Such an answer should be presented to modern scientists with the query: "Is your disbelief based on investigation or only on a passive second-hand acceptance of fashionable scepticism based on the prestige of science and technology?"

Suggestions and social prestige based on the achievements of science in the making of motor cars or even space vehicles or inter-continental missiles or jet planes are no automatic disproof of the influence of stars and planets on the life of man. This point of view that each branch of science and art should be judged by the evidence suited to it and not be condemned out of court has been gaining ground in the second half of the twentieth century.

In fact it is no exaggeration to say that we have now in the world of science, letters and culture generally, a veritable renaissance of astrology and related views favouring faith in the unseen or spiritual aspects of reality, internal and external.

There are emerging scientists and investigators who are quietly gathering data and testing them in various fields. Scientific method is being applied to probe the world of astrological phenomena—the positions of the planets and stars and their influence on lives. The old dogmatism is giving way.

Astrology is standing out as a distinct science and art based on proved astronomical facts and is being differentiated from popular palmistry, crystal gazing, thought-reading and jugglery.

It will be seen from the arguments adduced, and the facts presented in the following pages, that none of the *a priori* objections to the idea of a relation between astronomical phenomena and terrestrial happenings—an unpleasant deduction but a fact objectively established—is seriously tenable.

As scientific investigation exhausts its curiosity and reduces the relationship in the field of material phenomena, inevitably comes the necessity of considering higher relationships, due to the fact that man himself is not a mechanical automation but is endowed with will and intelligence. Astrology in respect of its universal application is a field of enquiry too extensive for little more than surface consideration.

A careful consideration of the evolution of human thought in the West reveals three broad epochs in man's efforts to understand the workings of nature. They are animistic, mechanical and mathematical. As Sir James Jean writes: "The animistic period was characterised by the error of supposing that the course of nature was governed by the whims and passions of living beings, more or less like man himself. Because personality is the concept of which he has most immediate and direct experience, he begins by personifying everything."

Jeans goes on to say: [1]"As the history of the individual is merely the history of the race writ small, our race did much the same in its infancy as its individuals still do in theirs Greek science consisted in the main of mere vague questionings and speculations as to why things came to be as they were rather than the otherwise."

So long as men could only experiment with objects which were comparable in size, with their own bodies, they found *inanimate nature* behaving as though its constituent pieces exerted pushes and pulls to one another. This mechanistic view of

1 *New Background of Science.*

nature in its turn implies absolute determinism and explained the workings of nature in terms of the familiar concepts of everyday life. Today, however, as Jeans says, [2]"we are beginning to see that man had freed himself from the anthropomorphic error of imagining that the workings of nature could be compared to those of his own whims and caprices (animism), only to fall headlong into the second anthropomorphic error of imagining that they could be compared to the workings of his own muscles and sinews (mechanism)."

It must be noted that even modern scientists fall into the same error of thinking that Jeans has charged the mechanists and the animist with, because whilst the animists and the mechanists proceeded in the same general lines as the child and the unreflective savage, the modern scientist has built an inferential world out of the impressions gathered through his senses and instruments. The scientist feels that which is not convincing to him or possible to him would be and must be so to the rest of mankind. To think that phenomenon which is inexplicable to him, must be so to the rest of mankind is to argue like a fool. To the ancient Hindus goes the credit of having discovered some of the fundamental laws governing the universe and its inhabitants. [3]"The

2 *New Background of Science.*

3 *Hindu Astrology* by Mankari Pande.

sages possessed a much more accurate, dependable and comprehensive instrument with which to observe natural phenomenon—their ability to function in what might be called a fourth dimensional consciousness or Yoga—which enabled them to note, to measure, to weigh and to classify all the facts concerning the universe without micro meters and telescopes." This super-consciousness which they required, to put in Prof. B. Suryanarain Rao's words, "by intensifying the sense-energies internally according to approved yogic methods" made them "aware of and able to comprehend infinitesimal units of time and space too small to be measured by the most modern scientific instruments and vast spans of years and universes, too remote to be found even by the largest telescope". Concentration of the mind yields more valuable results than the employment of laboratory methods with a mind that is incapable of intuition or internal development. What Einstein and Eddington have said about the universe, and what they have yet to say about man's relation to universe, the Maharshis have already said. Their conclusions are neither animistic nor mechanistic nor mathematical. The scientist keeps his nose fixed to his mathematical formulae, seeking to divine the structure of the material universe. But the Maharshis were not blind to the so-called unknown forces which lie back of material phenomena. They found out the grand truth that man is the reflection of the universe. The key to understand this fundamental truth lies in astrology.

Scientists have been rapidly changing their views and outlook upon external nature, and have begun to tread the domain of Hindu philosophy by propounding strange concepts of space, time and matter, while psychologists are becoming more and more conscious of the fact that mind can wield direct influence on the outer world, a secret known to the Hindus long before the period of so-called dawn of scientific knowledge. Wherever the scientist looks at, he is confronted with the mystery of life with the result he has been practically groping in the dark. Unless he recognises the importance of astrology, the fundamental problems about man and his place in the universe must always remain a mystery. Astrology takes into cognisance the relation existing between man and the cosmos.

We have said above that Western scientific thought could be divided into three broad epochs, *viz.*, animistic, mechanistic and mathematical. These three correspond also to the three stages of astrological thought. In the beginning, astrology dealt with the planetary bodies mainly as entities fit to be worshipped and this animistic attitude still remains as an important feature of remedial astrology. The 'animism' here is only an euphemism and has nothing in common with 'animism' of the West. The second stage of astrological thought concerned itself to an elucidation of the "periodicity of life-process"—the mechanism of science—corresponding in terms of material activity. In the third stage, astrology served as a means to bring biological and [4]"psychological order into the inner natures of men who had been unbalanced". Recently electricity and radioactivity led man to the startling concepts of twentieth century physics—the new world of thought, widely open to the unknown and it is astrology that should supply the key to the unknown and unknowable.

"The law of analogy presupposes a Universal Agent permeating the entire universe"—a life substance—comic energy—filling in all space. It is now being increasingly realised that a certain 'phase of relationship exists between man's conscious ego and Nature. At some time these were held to be physiological and elemental. Now they are to be psychological and mental. And astrology integrates and correlates this principle of order".

Science is beginning to realise that [5]"we are now faced with a cosmic determinism in which our free-

---

4 *Astrology of Personality* by Dane Rudhyar.

5 "Astrology and Modern Science," by O. B. Vijayamuni, in The Astrological Magazine for May 1946.

doms become illusions, as misleading as our rages and fears, which we think are volitions but which are registered even when the cerebral cortex has been surgically removed". The law of Karma and its relation to astrology have a direct bearing upon the theory of 'determinism' which modern thinkers could have developed further if the doctrines enumerated thousands of years ago by the Hindus had been taken note of. It is only by assuming that determinism in some form or other exists in nature that prediction can become possible. According to Laplace there is a law in nature that "like causes produce like effects". This means some sort of determinism exists suggesting thereby nature's uniformity. Haldane whilst criticising Laplace in this regard does not doubt the possibility of "a very high degree of accuracy in the prediction both of physical and social happenings". Bertrand Russel concedes that [6]"a correlation which has been found true in a number of cases, and has never been found false, has at least a certain assignable degree of probability of being always true". This definition is of great importance to students of astrology. The above statements automatically lead to the acceptance of 'determinism'. Unless there is some sort of a cause-effect principle, prediction, even to the extent Russel suggests, would be impossible. Planck

---

6 *Analysis of Matter.*

honestly confesses that the "knowable realities of nature cannot be exhaustively discovered by any branch of science" and that "this means that *science is never in a position completely and exhaustively to explain the problems it has to face*". Professor Einstien is stated to have observed: "Honestly I cannot understand what people mean when they talk about the freedom of the human will." Schopenhauer said that "man can do what he wills but he cannot will what he wills".

Planck's discovery of Quantum Theory is supposed to have disturbed the principle of determinism or causality. The materialist believes that chance and necessity explain natural phenomena. It should occur to any man of average intelligence that blind chance in nature is meaningless, because it cannot explain any natural phenomena satisfactorily. We do not wish to enlarge this question further because it belongs to the province of dialectics and involves profound thinking. Suffice it to say that cool reflection reveals the operation of some *intelligent design* throughout the universe. This grand truth was perceived by the Sages through intuition or introspection, a process as reliable in its possibilities as it is difficult of achievement by the modern scientist.

The next shock the law of determinism is supposed to have received was from the discovery of

Rutherford that [7]"atoms at times disintegrate themselves spontaneously and at times behave in a different way". Bohr found out [8]"that the electron of the atom does not travel uniformly in a continuous stream but by jumps". The impact of these discoveries on the theory of causality was considerable because they demonstrated that [9]"nature had hardly any such law of uniformity". This was followed by Heisenberg's new Quantum Mechanics according to which [10]"although there occur sudden breaks and jumps in the motion, still they are so minute at times that the effect for all practical purposes is continuous and uniform". In other words, according to the Sanskrit maxim "*dhatanam yatat purvama kalaayet*" (there is nothing new on the surface of the earth), scientific concepts, after the investigations of Planck, Einstein and Heisenberg, are going back to the same old theories from which they started. Eddington warns us thus in a beautiful manner: "There is nothing new under the Sun and this latest *Volte Face* almost brings us back to Newton's theory of light—a curious mixture of corpuscular and wave theory. There is perhaps a pleasing sentiment in this return to Newton".

---

7 *Materialism, Marxism, Determinism and Dialectics* by Das Gupta
8 *Ibid.*
9 *Ibid.*
10 *Ibid.*

It will be seen that all the rude shocks that determinism is supposed to have received was only in the realm of the atom and the electron. If we take a human being we find that some sort of determinism exists. Even indeterminate events are governed by statistical laws. "Laws can be found which can govern the behaviour of crowds of electrons". In regard to man the past and present can indicate the future, let us say, generally, though not precisely. We need not be carried away by the hue and cry of the scientist about the breakdown of determinism because his reference is only to the atomic world. Fundamental things still exist beyond man's understanding.

We have said elsewhere that the ancient Maharshis discovered grand truths the fringe of which Einstein and Eddington have just now reached, by deep mental concentration. Concentration of mind presupposes complete detachment. Without such detachment, 'investigation' into the realm of the unknown is not possible. Does the modern scientist have this power of detachment? Heisenberg has proved that the "investigator *does* affect the investigation and that there is no getting away from this fact". As long as the scientist is unable to bring to bear upon his investigations 'pure mind and pure thought' his conclusion, which may be true in atomic matters, can never be accepted as true in social and historical matters. The marvellous achievement of having soared into the mysterious regions of the abstract by 'pure thought' and discoverd one great fundamental truth belongs to those great Maharshis like Vyasa, Kanada and Kapila.

[11]"In their process of thinking, they had an extraordinary dynamic power of assimilating ideas." That the Maharshis' findings are to be accepted as authoritative seems as if echoed by no less a person than the great scientist Heisenberg when he observes thus : "Many of the abstractions that are characteristic of modern theoretical physics to be found discussed in the philosophy of past centuries. At that time these abstractions could be disregarded as mere mental exercises by those scientists whose only concern was with reality but today we are compelled by the refinements of experimental art to consider them seriously."

In the face of such a bold assertion on the part of Heisenberg, it is strange that the metaphysical speculations of the Upanishads and the Acharyas should still be anathema to the scientific man of today. As Dr. Rhine observes, [12]"there is an unfortu-

11 *Materialism, Marxism, Determinism and Dialectics* by Das Gupta.
12 *Reach of the Mind.*

nate taboo both in the school and out of it against discussion of beliefs concerning man's ultimate nature".

Every advance in scientific research, every new discovery of natural law, whether in the realm of chemistry or biology, means a real extension of the deterministic principle, which in its turn implies some sort of causal line. Bertrand Russel observes thus : [13]"I call a series of events a causal line, if given some of them we can infer something about the others without having to know anything about the environment." In other wards the possibility of prediction is conceded. I must warn readers that I am deliberately omitting to use the term 'Fate' though both Fate and Determinism connote more or less the same idea. I shall subsequently deal with the question of Fate and Freewill and their relation to astrology.

One of the reasons for the degeneration of astrology appears to be due to the fact that the scientific mind became more or less an analytical machine. Man has become too selfish and sensuality, mental chaos and intellectual perversion have become deeply rooted. Astrology [14]"perforce ceased to be vital and necessary to the collectivities as a principle of order because the growing domination of the

13 *Human Knowledge, Its Scope and Limits.*

14 *Astrology of Personality* by Dane Rudhyar.

intellectual rational principle enabled man to project speculatively his own order into the world". The biological order is indeed of a different kind. The intellect which is but an instrumentality helping man to raise his consciousness [15]"creates a separative kind of individualism based on analysis..............As individuals became more and more the important thing," astrology descended itself to the level of fortune-telling. The deeper phases of astrology found themselves reborn only after the late Prof. B. Suryanarain Rao entered the field and took up its cause.

The situation now in the trend of scientific thought is extremely confusing. We may therefore conclude that in regard to all human events some sort of determinism does exist while in the atomic world "determinism of a statistical kind exists".

While causalism and mechanism have been valuable adjuncts in the study of physical phenomena, they have done nothing to explain the psychological phenomena. Since astrology is concerned as much with the physical aspect of man as it is with his psychological aspect, a few observations on the values of time seem to be necessary. Since the causality principle appeared inadequate to explain psychological phenomena the great psychologist

---

15 *Astrology of Personality* by Dane Rudhyar.

Jung found that [16]"there are psychic parallelisms which cannot be related to each other causally, but which must be connected through another sequence of events". Jung goes on to say : [17]"This connection seemed to me to be essentially provided in the fact of the relative simultaneity, therefore the expression synchronistic". Time contains, according to Jung, "qualities or basic conditions manifesting simultaneously in various places in a way not to be explained by causal parallelisms, as for example, in cases of the coincident appearance of identical thoughts, symbols or psychic conditions". In a personal letter addressed to me (the full text of which appears in the Appendix) Dr. Jung has conceded the validity of astrology. As regards the basis of astrology, he does not give a correct picture inasmuch as he thinks that correct astrological deductions "are not due to the effect of constellations, but to our hypothetical time charecters". Evidently Carl Jung does not appear to have been aware of the Hindu point of view in regard to prediction. The future is a reflection of the past. The horoscope simply indicates the future. But the so-called influence of a planet or a star is only a proximal case. We may not subscribe to the views of Jung in their entirety.

---

16 *Secret of the Golden Flower.*

17 *Ibid.*

They are quoted to the extent needed to support astrological thought. As the 'synchronistic' principle represents a time evaluation and "based on the formative potency of the moment," it is closely, though not entirely, allied to the astrological precept. Planets are manifestation of matter and they move in space. Their movements are regulated in time. Therefore astrology connects time, space and matter together and demonstrates the synchronistic as well as causality or deterministic principles. It is an art of life-interpretation and provides us with a technique of self-improvement and perfection.

That there is determinism as often as there is indeterminism in the atomic world leads us to think that on the one hand there is the inevitable effect of Karma, and that on the other hand there is Freewill also.

II

ASTROLOGY AND KARMA

It is in this way that the Maharshis propounded the grand law of Karma and Rebirth. If the theory of rebirth is not accepted it is not possible to explain the destiny of man and all the differences and disparities in spite of apparently equal does of effort and will. Environmental conditions and economic factors may explain the disparity to some extent. Where we cannot explain things with reason, we at once bring in the name of chance, *a safety valve* to conceal our ignorance. In the absence of causality or determinism, chance or accident is the only explanation. A problem whose explanation requires great thinking should not be disposed of out of an accident. On the contrary, the inequities, differences and distinctions compelled the sages to accept the theory of Karma. In physical phenomena the cause and effect relationship can easily be demonstrated but in regard to Karma theory the effect of action cannot be physically analysed. It is a conception, indeed a grand conception. based on sound logic. The law of Karma operates through a series of births. Man has to suffer the consequences of his actions until he succeeds in regulating his actions by true knowledge and wisdom. To the Hindus this [18]"karma theory and freewill are not creations of a fanciful imagination" or false solace. They are demonstrated facts—demonstrated in the sense that the Sages in a state of spiritual ecstacy did realise their truth. A critical mind will be able to see that there is a striking resemblance between a pure thought (yogic introspection of the Maharshis) and the laboratory investigation. The latter has shown that in regard to the atomic world 'determinism' and 'indeterminism' obtain while the Maharshis have shown that when once a man "has done an act he must get the inevitable result of his own action", and that "there is a freewill to act or not to act, but once the act is done, the law of Karma will bring its own result. There is no escape from the inevitable consequence of action but by exercise of freewill, man may guide his future and thereby create his own destiny". Astrology or *Hora Sastra* reveals the result of our past karma, expressed probably in terms of what we crudely call planetary influences.

Astrology and Karma are therefore interrelated. Astrology reveals the consequence of our actions

---

18 *Materialism, Marxism, Determinism and Dialectics* by Das Gupta.

which we do not remember in this life and are untraceable in this birth. The result of our unknown actions is what we call 'fate' or *adrishtra*. The law of Karma therefore indicates the cause and effect relationship.

Before taking up the significance of astrology, we have to make a few more remarks about the law of Karma. Many people imagine that the theory of Karma is based on fatalism and predestined necessity and that, therefore, it leaves no scope for individual development. Such a misconception is partly due to the ignorance of the theory of Karma. One must admit that the universe is either cosmos or chaos ; it cannot be partly ruled by law and partly by chance. The experiences of generations of thinkers should convince any intelligent person that the universe and the life activities are regulated by certain laws. If the Sun and the planetary bodies are subject to discipline and their movements and phenomena are according to a certain order, then the lives of individuals who inhabit the planetary systems must also be guided by certain definite laws and rules, and chance cannot make one a king and the other a beggar by the mere accident of birth.

"For the study of Karma, it is best to consider the man at the level of his individuality or 'soul'. The soul is said to be immortal. Only the so-called positivists and some allied schools of thought doubt the immortality of the soul. A conscious existence after death has no better proof than a pre-natal existence. It is an old declaration that what begins in Time must end in Time. We have no right to say that the soul is eternal on one side of its earthly period without being so on the other. Far more rational is the view of certain scientists, who believing that the soul originates with this life also declare that it ends with this life. That is the logical outcome of their premise. If the soul sprang into existence specially for this life, why should it continue afterwards? It is precisely as probable from all the grounds of reason that death is the conclusion of the soul as that birth is the beginning of it. It was this argument which had special weight with the Greek philosophers whose reasonings upon immortality have led all later European generations. They asserted the eternity of soul in order to vindicate its immortality. The Hindu conception is of course more profound. Man's existence, says one of the disciples of Kapila, the first evolutionist in the world, is a mere repetition of his other previous existences. His present existence is but a link in the chain of eternal existences connecting the past with the future. In his each birth, he carries one step forward, the inceptive purpose of his creation to its goal and consummation until it attains the one in which the past, present and future are blended together and time and space annihilated. Above all, our instinctive belief in immortality implies a sub-conscious acceptance of this view. If we do not grant the immortality of the soul, the inconceivability of annihilation or of creation from nothing becomes obvious. Granting the permanence of the human 'spirit', 'soul', 'ego', 'atman'—whatever you call it—the law of Karma is the only one yielding a metaphysical explanation of the phenomenon of life. It is already accepted in the physical plane as evolution and holds a firm ethical value in applying the law of justice to human experience.

The law of Karma suggests, that our actions—physical as well as psychical—are performed according to certain regular laws with a definite end in view. Actions performed may fructify in a minute, or in a day, or in a year, or in one life, or in several lives. Actions, when performed, remain in the form of something unseen till the time of their fructification and during this period this something is known as 'adrishta' (the so-called luck or fortune). There is no escape without the experience of the fruits of these actions—(desires and thoughts)—until the whole adrishta is exhausted.

Feelings of pleasure and pain and like and dislike characterise all our activities in any walk of life.

This cannot be denied. Ancient writers say that these feelings cannot be attributed to external things; for an external thing or object which gives pleasure to a man at one particular time causes pain to the same man at another time instead of producing pleasure at all times. Hence the (material not the instrumental) cause is traced to the 'soul' which is the seat of these feelings. Since the 'soul' is eternal, it cannot be the requisite cause, because if it were the requisite cause, the effect ought to have been ever present, which is not the fact. Hence, the presence of a determining factor to the Atma is necessary. The ancient Hindu schools believed in the existence of an unseen force, which is called *Dharma-dharma* or 'adrishta' or the sum-total of Karma. It is this unseen force which helps the fructification of the deeds of the past.

According to ancient texts when one dies, his soul which is enveloped in a subtle body and invested with the sum-total of good and bad Karma passes after some time into another body leaving off his gross body, as a man casts off worn-out clothes and puts on new ones. His reincarnation takes place in a physical body corresponding with the deeds done by him in his previous life. The processes of death and birth go on until the person concerned attains emancipation. The cardinal doctrine of Karma therefore is the law of cause and effect in accordance with the maxim "as a man soweth so shall he reap". The Darwinian theory of evolution is defective inasmuch as it does not offer a satisfactory solution of the problems agitating the human mind from times immemorial. The Darwinian theory of evolution stops with man. Karma theory on the other hand takes us further and says that according to the maxim 'action and reaction are equal and opposite', when there is evolution there must necessarily be devolution also. Hence a Brahmin in this life may be born as a Harijan in the next life ; a rich man in this life may be born as a poor man in the next life and *vice versa.* Thus the station of life or the degree of wealth, etc., that one has attained in this life is mostly due to the Karma at his credit in the previous life. Karma is due to our actions and our actions are due to our thoughts. Hence it is man who creates his Karma for it is the product of his thought.

There are three categories of Karma, *viz.,* (1) Sanchita, (2) Prarabdha and (3) Agami. The Sanchita or accumulative Karma pertains to actions that are still lying latent "like seeds stocked up in a granary for fruition in future lives." The present course of life is indicated by the Prarabdha or operative Karma, deeds or actions whose seed has already sprung up and whose machinery has been set in motion towards their fruition in the present life. Agami pertains to actions contemplated to be done. There are several gradations of Karma suggested in Hindu philosophical and astrological works and these details do not concern us now.

[19]"It would further seem that man is responsible only for such acts as are generated in the mind. He is not responsible for actions where the thought or intent did not run with the deed. For instance, in turning quickly on a station platform some one bumps into a person standing behind him as a result of which the latter falls in front of a train; the former would not be responsible for death which he never intended. Here the law would seem to be the 'above' of which English law is the reflected, though unconsciously reflected 'below'. For in English law, there must, to constitute responsibility, not only be an *actus reus*, the wrongful deed, but also a *mens rea*, the wicked mind." This however is a very general comparison. Prof. B. Suryanarain Rao observes thus: [20]"Before the birth of a child, it has some Karma to its credit and as the result of that Karma it takes birth in a particular family with particular surroundings, special physical features and noticeable mental inclinations. This Karma of the infant which resulted in its birth and surroundings is called *Sanchita* or that which already was stored in, by this child before

---

19 *Karma and Rebirth* by Christian Humphreys.

20 *An Introduction to Astrology* by B. S. Rao.

the present birth, to its credit. *Pararbdha* is that which it does after the birth. Here is a grand mystery in nature which requires deep and intelligent study to understand it. Some of the actions of the child are due to its predilections for certain things, as being the results of past Karma. But the child has a will of its own. This is partly under the control of the past karmic results and partly independent of them, like the mystery of the nails. These nails are apparently dead, but they are also living for they grow, but they can be cut, carved or burnt without any pain to a certain extent. How dead matter can grow out of living matter is a mystery which can only be understood by a higher person who is on grander intellectual planes? When the child does an act as the result of its previous Karma, it must be attributed to Sanchita or stored-up Karma. But when it does something in its life by the semi-independent will, the Karma will be characterised as Prarabdha or that which is done in the present state of existence. But when a man says that he will kill a person next year, or commit adultery with a girl after she attains her age, or do charity when he gets rich, the Karma has yet to be done, and this will be classified as Agami. This again may be the result of past Karma and present will-force, joined together or may be due to other mysterious forces.

"Thus each of the divisions of Karma, *viz.*, Sanchita, Prarabdha and Agami has again to be subdivided into three classes. All human actions may be brought together under (1) Kayaka—bodily, (2) Vachaka—pertaining to speech, and (3) Manasika—mental influences. A man does something by his body, such as kicking, beating, squeezing, embracing, etc., and all these physical actions are called kayaka or pertaining to the kaya or body. All those actions which he does by speech are called vachaka and these are stronger than the first set of kayaka or bodily actions. Then there are the actions of mind, thinking good or evil and these are classed as manasika or mental. As mind power is the grandest yet discovered in all nature, actions of the mind are the most powerful and surpass in intensity all other kinds of actions. Sanchita, therefore, as well as Prarabdha and Agami, has three sorts of Karma attached to it and here come the complications of Karma theory."

Karma theory teaches us that soul enters this life, not as a fresh creation, but after a long course of previous existences on this earth and elsewhere, in which it acquired its present inhering peculiarities and that it is on the way to future transformations which the soul is now shaping. It claims that infancy brings to earth, not a blank scroll for the beginning of an earthly record, nor a mere cohesion of atomic forces into a brief personality soon to disclose again into the elements, but that it is inscribed with ancestral histories, some like the present scene the most of them unlike it and stretching back into, and remotest past. These inscriptions are generally undecipherable, save as revealed in their moulding influence upon the new career, but like the invisible photographic images made by the Sun of all it sees; when they are properly developed in the laboratory of consciousness, they will be distinctly displayed. The current phase of life will also be stored away in the secret vaults of memory for its unconscious effect upon ensuing lives. All the qualities we now possess in body, mind and soul result from our use of ancient opportunities. we are indeed the heirs of all the ages. For these conditions accrue from distant causes endangered by our older selves, and the future flows by the divine law of cause and effect (Karma) from the gathered momentum of our past impetuses. There is no favoritism in the universe, but all have the same everlasting facilities for growth. Those who are now elevated in worldly station may be sunk in humble surroundings in the future. Only the inner traits of the soul are permanent companions. The wealthy sluggard may be the beggar of the next life, and the industrious worker of the present is sowing the seeds of greatness. Suffering, bravely endured now, will produce a treasure of patience and fortitude in another life, hardships will give rise to strength, self-denial must develop the will, tastes cultivated in this existence will somehow bear fruit in coming ones and acquired energies will assert themselves whenever they can by the *less parsimoniae* upon which the principles of physics are based. *Vice versa*, the unconscious habits, the uncontrollable impulses, the peculiar tendencies, the favourite pursuits, and the soul-stirring friendships of the present descend from far-reaching previous activities.

Karma is what we have done, and we have to enjoy the karmic results. Therefore it follows that the *future* is only the *past*. It should threfore be possible to predict the future. The astrologer feels by means of his art the cloud of unexpended Karma in the aura and tries to read it. Planets therefore simply indicate the results of previous Karma and hence there is nothing like fate or destiny in its absolute sense controlling us. "The indications of planets are something like *show cause* notices of a legal court. The sections mentioned therein are technical and they indicate with what sort of commission or omission of duty the person is charged with. He must make preparations to meet them. Thus a man borrows unduly from another and fails to pay him. This will bring a decree against the defaulter and a notice will issue for its execution. The decree does not prohibit the defaulter from earning money by any means and paying it off or going to the creditor and satisfying his demands by other means, such as personal service, intercessions of relations or friends, pleading for mercy, etc. Similarly the planets indicate the evil or good results of the previous Karma and leaves it to man to counteract them or allow them to have their full sway. Thus the good or bad Sanchita Karma at our credit can be augmented or minimised by the Prarabdha Karma with the aid of will-power, which is limitless in its potentiality." Astrology therefore does not lead to a weakening of the will. Science explains the idiosyncrasies of plants and animals by the environment of previous generations, and calls instinct, hereditary habit. In the same way there is an evolution of individuality, by which the child opens its new era with characteristics derived from anterior lives and adds the experience of a new personality to the sum-total of his treasured traits. In its passage through earthly personalities the spiritual self, the essential ego, accumulates a fund of individual character, which remains as the permanent thread stringing together the separate lives. The soul is therefore an eternal water globule, which sprung in the beginningless past from mother ocean and is destined after an unreckonable course of meanderings in cold and rain, snow and steam, spring and river, mud and vapour, to at last return with the garnered experience of all lonely existences into the central heart of all.

That we have forgotten the causes producing the present sequences of pleasures and paids, talents and defects, successes and failures is no disproof of them, and does not disturb the justice of the scheme. For temporary oblivion is the anodyne by which the kindly physician is bringing us through the darker wards of sorrow into perfect health.

The law of Karma provides a graded sanction or reason for right living. It proves that men are in essence one, and that any deed which hurts one's neigbourhood or the commonweal is an injury to oneself. Above all, it reveals a plane of consciousness where right becomes the inmost law of being and a man does right not because it pays or becase it avoids self-injury, but because, beyond all argument, he must. Karma destroys the cause of envy and the consequent ill-will. It removes impatience. It largely removes the fear of death for which there is the inner conviction of rebirth and by the law of affinity re-union with those one loves, why worry.

The belief in the theory of Karma and reincarnation scattered through the philosophical writings of India reproduce the scientific theories of the involution and evolution of the elements. The swarming millions of India have made the thought 'the soul is older than body' the foundation of their enormous achievements in Government, philosophy, architecture and poetry. Throughout the East, it is the great central thought. It is no mere superstition of the ignorant masses. It is the chief principle of Hindu metaphysics—the basis of all their inspired books. Such a hoary philosophy, held by the venerable authority of the ages, ruling from the beginning of time the bulk of the world's thought, cherished in some form by the disciples of every great religion, is certainly worthy of the profoundest respect and study.

The conceit of modern progress has no more respect for ancient ideals than for the forgotten civilisation of old, even though in many essentials they have anticipated or out-stripped all that we boast of.

In this connection a reference may be made to the observations of Lakhovsky on immortality and reincarnation. He has made a new approach to these great problems in the sense, he explains the concepts on a material and biological basis. According to his doctrine of *Materialisation* and *Dematerialisation* the process of creation and disappearance of matter is perpetually going on. "Through condensation cosmic rays are transformed into electrons, atoms and molecules, and inversely in radioactivity, we witness the transformation of matter into radiation." In his book *Matter* Lakhovsky explains how rays from one star can enter resonance with chromosomes in living beings dwelling on another planet or star and give birth to life. In other words, he suggests that life can be continuously converged through radiation from one planet to the other, or from the earth to another planet or star. By this process, he thinks we live physically eternally through materialisation of radiations. Readers must be aware that according to Hindu astrology, in studying the 5th house, we are asked to ascertain the fertility or otherwise of the couple by a consideration of what are called *beeja* and *kshetra* representing, as they do, not merely the sperm and the ovum but the *element* which really makes the male and female fluids fertile or suitable for the entry of a new soul. The husband and wife may be physiologically normal. Their sex-relations may be happy. But still if their *beeja* and *kshetra* are not strong, when judged according to astrological rules, they will not bring forth any issues. This want of 'fertility' in the seed or the bed derives a rational explanation from Lakhovsky, for he "claims that the act of fertilisation between the sexes is itself insufficient to produce the living being ....It is necessary that when fertilisation occurs, at this moment certain cosmic radiations materialise within the fertilised egg". Whether or not in all human beings such materialisation occurs, could be ascertained astrologically by the beeja and kshetra method.

Lakhovsky observes :

[21]"We all know, besides, that fertilisation often does not occur until the end of several months and even after several years. This delay of impregnation may be due to the specific radiations of the male or female, which are not always in resonance with the radiation of *materialisation*. The organism from the first cell, in its development, is thus materialisation of rays transmitted by its other ego on another planet, and continues during its development to evolve under the domination of the same specific complex of radiations coming from the being that originally gave it life. They transmit to it, by its own vibration, during its entire existence, all the characteristics of its other ego dwelling on another planet.

"All this explains how every living being (microbe, infusoria, plant, animal, man) reproduces itself to infinity on other planets, where its complex of radiations finds favourable conditions of resonance

---

21 *Eternity, Life and Death*

and so materialise themselves in various parts of the universe to eternity. These materialisations, by the propagation of the radiations from planet to planet, can repeat themselves indefinitely, in the infinity of time and space. The life of every being, including man, on all planets is nothing but the result or materialization produced by successive and eternal resonances.

"It thus follows that all beings that lose their lives are not dead in reality, in the absolute sense of the word, but continue to live with their full consciousness in other regions of the universe. They could perfectly well be reborn on earth through a previous rematerialisation and relive with their bullness of their personality in flesh and bone. Also, we are simply reproductions by materialisation of beings existing or having existed on our earth or on other planets. So, great men who died in the past are not dead, but continue to live in flesh and bone, in full consciousness, on other planets, and they continue their work.

"This reincarnation of human beings on other stars can explain certain facts otherwise difficult to account for. Thus how can we understand the extraordinary aptitudes of a man of genius born of mediocre parents ? The laws of heredity seem superseded and are powerless to account for the exceptional qualities of this man. On the contrary, everything is explained by the effect of the transmission of a complex of human rays through space, at the moment of conception. This being of genius is formed by the process (of materialization of cellular radiations travelling through space from planet to planet) indicated above, thanks to the union of the united gametes with rays of the same characteristic rate of vibration coming from another exceptional individual who died on some distant star.

"Thus great thinkers, great artists, great philosophers, great statesmen, and all other geniuses of which history has transmitted their names, are, in all probability, repetitions of other thinkers, artists, philosophers and statesmen who have died on other stars or on the earth".

Indicating that the birth of such individuals must occur at times when stellar and planetary vibrations are harmonious to their own rate of vibration, Lakhovsky concludes :

[22]"There is yet another reason why we should not put aside without profound examination the theories that place special importance to the marked influence on human destiny of the position of the stars in the heaven at the moment of conception and

---

22 *Eternity, Life and Death.*

birth of a human being. I have elsewhere dealt with the question of the influence of the position of the stars in my books, *The Secret of Life,* and *Eternity, Life and Death*".

Lakhovsky clearly upholds the theory of astrology by his able and scholarly expositions bearing on cosmic radiations and their influences on terrestrial affairs.

III

WHAT IS ASTROLOGY?

Some people define astrology as the science of stars. Others say that it is the art by which the future of man can be known. It may also be defined as "the philosophy of discovering and analysing past impulses and future actions of both individuals and nations" in the light of planetary configurations. Astrology explains life's reactions to planetary vibrations. In Sanskrit, it is called Hora Sastra or Jyotisha or the Science of Time. All these definitions do not convey a correct idea of the subject. It is much more than a science. It is a science of the sciences, the key to all knowledge. It is the knowledge that links man to nature and establishes that order regins supreme in life and that chance and accident have no place. Astrology can be defined as the science of correlation of astronomical facts with terrestrial events. The celestial bodies are conspicuous by the presence of supreme order in their revolutions. While this is the case could chaos exist on the earth and its phenomena? Astrology gave the answer that by juxtaposition of celestial order with terrestrial phenomena, the possibility of making prognostications could not be doubted. When an apparent effect is the resultant of a cause, then astrology becomes a symbol of measurement. The effect of a cause is expressed in terms of what we may call planetary influences.

Astrology is primarily concerned with the application of cosmic laws to terrestrial phenomena in general and man in particular. Hence pure objective science cannot lay down the law for astrology which deals with a different sphere of experience. Much less can it deny its very subject-matter or its relevance for human life or place in human culture which is concerned in the last resort with the art of life, utilising every facet of experience derived from objective nature and its effect on human life.

Astrology resembles history in an essential respect as a science. History is the science of human events in the past, ascertained and interpreted in accordance with tested methods such as those of observation, testimony, examination of MSS, coins, historical monuments, documents, etc. The method is scientific in the sense of being methodical and systematic, using verification wherever possible. Interpretation uses human psychology—the motivations of historical personages and of the probabilities in the conduct of masses of men

Experimental verification in the sense that it is possible in a chemical laboratory is not of course possible in history nor even in contemporary sociology, for human beings cannot be experimented upon like guinea pigs (though it may sometimes be attempted in a totalitarian system of Government). Verification is possible in astrology to the extent it is possible in history and sociology.

For instance, astrology reveals correspondences between the afflictions of Mars in a man's horoscope and his bodily illness or an affliction of Saturn in the 12th house is accompanied by deafness or ear troubles. Similarly eye diseases appear in a man simultaneously with afflictions in certain stars in his horoscope—Jyeshta or Antares.

Sometimes doubters in astrology go further and ask how such correspondences *can be true*.

The sense that such correspondences or effects of distant planetary bodies on human lives are impossible and contrary, to nature, or accepted view of nature, and of the cosmos, rests on unconsciously accepted assumptions about their nature and about the relations between them. But this assumption is arbitrary. There is no reason why the real inwardness of the heavenly bodies—planets and stars—and their mutual relations and their impact on human life and destiny should resemble the things and relations of ordinary experience—stocks and stones.

The ancients must have discovered the effects of planets on man by two methods, *viz.,* intuition and observation. The fiirst according to the sages is difinitely more trustworthy. Intuition, introspection or *divyadrishti* is an individual experience or perception or a faculty which the ancient Maharshis had acquired due to their austere and moral lives and by the practice of yoga. Bertrand Russel considers that "introspection is valid as a source of data, and is to a considerable extent amenable to scientific controls". Intuition transcends intellect. According to Jung, "intuition is a kind of instinctive appreciation irrespec tive of the nature of its contents. Through intuition any one content is presented as a complete whole. Intuitive cognition possesses an intrinsic nature of certainty and conviction which enabled Spinoza to uphold the *Scientia Intuitiva* as the highest form of cognition." Patanjali suggests in his famous *Yoga Sutras* that the Yogi, after reaching a certain plane of spiritual attainment, can establish direct communion with the different planetary bodies and perceive their mysteries without the aid of mechanical contrivances.

Observation must have played its part equally well. The sages must have noted the individual and collective events in the light of recurrence of certain planetary configurations, the psychological reactions of different types of people to certain planetary combinations. Hundreds of years of such observations must have convinced the sages that the birth in certain signs of the zodiac would confer certain definite psychological and physical traits. The planets, the signs and the zodiac became merely a symbol rendering possible the application of the laws of periodicity to individual and national lives.

The truth of astrology has also been established by statistical methods. As Bertrand Russel says, "Statistics ideally are accurate laws about large groups; they differ from other laws only in being about groups, not about individuals." Statistically it can be shown that several astrological combinations are corroborated. It will be seen that some of the greatest thinkers and intellectuals of all ages have endorsed the truth of astrology, and have consulted their horoscopes. The bard of Avon puts the following words into the mouth of King Lear:—

"It is the stars, the stars above us govern our condition.".

Even more striking is his flair for astrologic humour. He makes a disgruntled player to complain:

"It is impossible that anything should be as I would

have it; for I was born, Sir, when the Crab was ascending; and all my affairs go backwards."

Dante's astrology is written in majestic measure. We follow him into the vastness of space :

"..............................I saw
The sign that follows Taurus, and was in it.
Oh glorious stars ! Oh light impregnated
With mighty virtues, from which I acknowledge
All of my genius whatsoe'er it be,
With you was born, and hid himself with you
He who is father of all mortal life,
When first I tasted of the Tuscan air;
And then when grace was freely given to me
To enter the high wheel which turns you round
Your region was allotted unto me."[23]

[24]"For Dante astrology was the noblest of the sciences," writes H. Flanders Dunbar. "For Dante," she continues, "the principle of individualization is the influence of planets and stars, or, more accurately, of the intelligences by which they are moved. The ego, created directly by God, in its connection with the body comes under stellar influence, and at birth is stamped like wax by a seal. All impressions from the stars are good, since there is no lovableness that does not reflect the lovableness of God. It is the harmonizing and proportioning of these good

---

23 Paradiso, Canto XXII, *see* Hungad's *A Brief History of Astrology*
24 *Symbolism in Medieval Thought.*

qualities in their true relationships that make this or that person more or less perfect. It is likely that the modern reader, with his over-simple conception astrology, will lose much of the meaning of Dante...... Astrology was both more complicated and more scientific in the method than the familiar birth-month pamphlets suggest."

Goethe commits himself in no uncetain terms to both the theory and practice of astrology. He begins his autobiography thus : "On the 28th of August 1749, at midday, as the clock struck twelve, I came into the world, at Frankfort-on-the-Maine. The aspect of the stars was propitious ; the Sun stood in the sign of the Virgin, and had culminated for the day ; Jupiter and Venus looked on with a friendly eye, and Mercury not adversely ; the attitude of Saturn and Mars was neutral ; the Moon alone, just full, exerted all the more as her power of opposition had just reached her planetary hour. She, therefore, resisted my birth which could not be accomplished until this hour was passed. These auspicious aspects which the astrologers subsequently interpreted very favourably for me may have been the causes of my preservation."

Manly P. Hall observes thus : 'Let us suppose for a moment that the biographies of great men were to be written by scientists. The following might be a neat, brief and conservative treatise upon the subject, Abraham Lincoln : 'Abraham Lincoln, class mammalia, species homosapiens, was a body occupying place which integrated in 1809 and disintegrated in 1865. This body was presumably composed of approximately the following elements : Oxygen 65 per cent, carbon 18 per cent, hydrogen 10 per cent, nitrogen 3 per cent, calcium 2 per cent, phosphorus 1 per cent, the remaining 1 per cent being made up of small quantities of potassium, sodium, chlorine, magnesium, iron, iodine, fluorine and silicon. The type is peculiar to the planet earth.'

"This description of the Great Emancipator, though highly scientific and true to fact, nevertheless passes beyond the vanishing point of unimportance. The real Abraham Lincoln was an intellectual energy, a moral force, a courageous spirit, whose life and works profoundly influenced the course of civilization. Physicists might compute his specific gravity for ever and yet never discover Abraham Lincoln, the Man.

"In harmony with this viewpoint, we might hazard the speculation that astronomers have not yet '*discovered*' the intelligent universe. Though every element in cosmos be found and classified, the cosmos itself may still remain unknown. If astronomers say that Jupiter is a mass of gases, they but state a truth equally applicable to man. Yet, the average savant would scarcely rejoice in such a definition of himself. He would rather insist that his molecules and atoms have conspired to create a genius.

"It is quite scientific to presume that the universe bestowed all its intelligence upon man, leaving nothing but the mechanical qualities of rotation and revolution to be distributed among the suns, moons and stars—that race of giants which populates the firmament ? If human behaviour is intelligent, why is not universal behaviour intelligent ? If an insignificant mass of atoms on this earth could produce that Promethean soul of Abraham Lincoln, why should not a greater mass of atoms in the sky engender a still vaster spirit ? If no evidence of divine intelligence can be discovered in the chemical composition of the stars, it may be said with equal truth that no evidence of human intelligence can be discovered in the chemical composition of man. The ancient pagan belief that the stars were the bodies of Great beings replete with wisdom, who could be properly regarded as "divine", is no more unreasonable or inconsistent with science than to maintain that hydrogen and oxygen, together with thirteen other elements, when combined in the form of a college professor, are capable of propounding advanced problems in calculus.

"If, then, astrology postulates the heavenly bodies to be foci of intellectual energy, it claims nothing more unreasonable for the stars than that which is evident in man himself. By his benevolence or despotism, a single man can change the moral temper of civilization. History has demonstrated that a man may have an influence far beyond that which would seem consistent with the measure of his stature or its physical displacement. Furthermore, this personal force will communicate itself to future generations and continue as a dynamic impulse long after the man himself has been dissipated. Likewise the sidereal bodies, as parts of universal harmony or equilibrium, as factors in a balanced scheme, and modes of behaviour certainly constitute a heavenly environment, each contributing its physical ray to the rest and receiving into itself the moral electricity of brothers spheres".

Lawrence J. Benditt, an M.D. of Cambridge University and Phoebe D. Payne have argued that [25]"we are faced either with the fact that the extraordinarily accurate readings of astrological maps without the astrologer ever having seen the person are purely psychic or intuitive, or else with a mystery

---

25 *This World and That* : Chap, XI.

which goes deep down into the question of the relationship of man with the seeming objective world, whether as shown in the heavens or the more mundane sphere of everyday contacts. The fact, nevertheless, remains that even orthodox psychologists, some with a prejudice against such seemingly fantastic notions, have found themselves forced to realize that an expert astrologer can be of very real value in assessing the type and capacity of a person whose horoscope he has made. He can, for instance, predict such things as whether two people are likely to find marriage easy or difficult, creative or frustrating, whether there is a critical phase of life pending, and how the person concerned can best deal with it".

Tyrell believes [26]" that not only astrology, but the occult generally, is an obscure pointer to an aspect of the universe above, and beyond, the spatio-temproal ; Casual framework and the world of sense perception on which science has hitherto relied in its attempts to describe the objective universe".

---

26 *The Nature of Human Personality.*

IV

PLANETS AND MAN

Do planets influence man ? The reader can find an exhaustive answer in Prof. B. Suryanarain Rao's *Introduction to Astrology,* a masterpiece within its restricted scope. I shall only attempt to show that planets do *influence* terrestrial affairs. When the earth is called into its present shape by the solar influences, where is the logic of suggesting that bodies on its surface are not affected by them ? A trifling change in weather through solar causes brings neuralgia, headache, bronchitis, sore eyes, fever, smallpox, cholera, dysentery, plague and a host of other diseases too numerous to detail. War mania is a striking illustration of planetary influences. Our temper and moods depend upon the secretions of ductless glands. Fear is a matter of endocrine secretions ; indecision is a matter of thymus ; genius is a matter of thyroid. Sun's cycles of behaviour have their corresponding effects on these glands and their secretions and consequently on human behaviour. Each individual cell of our body is a living intelligent entity ; cells group according to the law of affinity and form tissue, the tissues form organs, each organ performing a function, all inter-dependent to a considerable extent. Thus every organ has 'intelligence', being composed of cells that know what to do and how to do it, and it is the intention of Nature that they shall perform their work perfectly, unless they meet interference —the principle of which is wrong suggestion. A being becomes cognisant of stimuli by the faculties of perception though the five senses, the main one of which is probably the sense of feeling. Feeling has a larger range than any of the other faculties. Not only can objective things be sensed by touch, but we can also feel invisible elements such as heat, cold and planetary vibrations. Planetary vibrations of varying character are continually exerting an influence which is taken up by our sensory nerves with the resulting bodily reactions, mental attitudes and moods. Therefore it is possible that solar, lunar and stellar energies supply the cells through the media of the nerves, their motivity. Different planetary vibrations—astrologically designated as yogas or aspects—supply different sensory stimuli, according as the vibrations differ in wavelengths, intensity, frequency, etc.

Amongst the researches of scientists who have studied the effects of sunspots and cosmic rays on human life and thereby accepted the basic principles of astrology, the most outstanding are those of the Russian biologist and physicist Prof. Georges Lakhovsky. He was perhaps the first modern scientist to openly state his belief that radiations from stars and planets can affect the future destiny of an individual at conception and birth. This reminds us of the great theory of the Maharshis about the importance of Adhana Lagna or conception time. If will be noted that Varahamihira propounded this truth two thousand years ago when European civilization was yet to be born. Professor Lakhovsky observes thus in his book *Le Grand P oblem* : "It is not without reason that the sages of antiquity intuitively attached great importance to the position of the stars in the sky at the moment of birth, for not only do the radiations from these stars exercise an influence on the animal and human embryo but, since all substance, living or inert, is constituted of electrons which are materialised radiations, the formation of all organic beings on earth depends directly on the influence of these radiations on the human egg at the moment of conception." In other words, Prof. Lakhovsky has shown that cosmic radiations pouring on the earth from outer space and coming from various stars and planets "act on the chromosomes of the cell nuclei which are cosmo-electrical resonators, absorb and take up these cosmic radiations, which are transformed into vital electricity and that mysterious force we call life. And in a similar manner he thinks that brain cells through antennae-like projections absorb stellar and planetary radiations just as radio antennae absorb radio waves."

According to Prof. Lakhovsky, "the gametes of the fertilised egg, which compose the chromosomes that determine hereditary characteristics, are altered to a specific wavelength at the time of conception and are capable of entering resonance with the radiations of the same vibratory rate coming from another planet or star." Consequently, observes the professor, "the ultra-microscopic field of force constituted by the combination of the gametes (in the fertilised egg) can enter into resonance with radiations coming from planets and stars having the same oscillatory character. This radiation could very well come from an individual who died ten, twenty, a hundred, a thousand or even a million years before on another celestial body, which harmonised with the ultra-microcosmic field of the gametes and which animates the egg, communicating its aptitudes, qualities and intellectual faults to the newly formed being." Here is much food for reflection when a scientist presents the revolutionary theory that the human being, from the moment of conception, is moulded by inpouring radiations from celestial bodies and that the destiny of the living organism is biologically sealed at birth.

The Sun is addressed in the Vedas as the soul of the universe. He is the visible God. Without Sun's heat and light nothing could exist in the world even for a single second. Varahamihira calls the Sun as *Kalatma* or the Soul of Time because Time exists only on account of the Sun. In fact, the Sun is the fountain-head of the life-force. The Sun's power is the cause of the cyclic motions of the earth and other planets. Sanskrit sciences call him as *Thrayee Thanu* or the three-souled as He is held to be the cause of bringing into existence, sustaining and finally destroying all terrestrial phenomena. *Bhoutikasutras* give different names to the Sun each connoting the nature of one of the aspects of His work in the scheme of evolution. For instance, one of the names suggested in *Bhoutikasutras* is Martanda. This is full of meaning. Maharshi Gobila says that Martanda implies the lending of the Power of dissolution to the universe at the time of Pralaya or annihilation and as the Sun is responsible for this, he would be the instrument of destruction and is therefore styled Martanda. Science has been seeking to unravel the mystery of the processes occurring on the Sun. A closer study of what are known as 'cosmic rays' would seem to hold out promise of reward. The secret of the cosmic rays will probably be found in the Sun, and Science will then be forced to admit what the great Maharshis have been proclaiming all these thousands of years that the real secret of the universe lies in the Sun. The Sun is also called Savita. Somasambhu a commentator of *Bhoutika-sutras*, opines that "*Suvanti*" is a life-force which joins all objects in nature, creates life-activity and helps creation. All objects in nature gain chaitanya or activity through *Suvanti* and since the Sun has this property in him, he is called *Savita*. We do not propose to enlarge upon this subject any more in this book.

The planets however are merely reflectors or transmitters of light and solar energy. The solar and planetary rays—radio-like waves—affect biological and psychological processes. The rays of influence are unseen vibrations. They are not perceptible to the physical eyes. Human sight has its limitations. It can observe things only that are vibrating between 481,000,000,000 and 764,000,000,000 vibrations per second. Therefore the rays of influence can be cognized by other senses and means. In fact, the assignment of astrological natures and characteristics to planets seems to have been based upon the vibrations theory. For instance, the vibrations of Saturn are slow, hence things of a corresponding nature are attributed to him. At first thought perhaps we find it difficult to believe in any direct influence between ourselves and the stars. But we must not lose sight of the fact that we are in electrical contact with the celestial bodies whose chemistry is ever changing. It is possible to calculate mathematically the attraction, say between Sun and the Earth. "Let M_1 and M_2 represent the masses of the two celestial bodies; D, the distance between them; and C, the gravitational constant, and equal to 1.069×10^9 poundals." The mass of the Sun is 1.9×10^{27} tons; the distance between the two bodies is 9.282×10^7 miles. Therefore the force of attraction between them is equal to $\frac{M_1 \times M_2}{D^2} \times C$

$$= \frac{(1.9 \times 10^{27} \times 2240)\,(5.87 \times 10^{21}) \times 1\,60 \times 10^9}{(9.282 \times 10^7 \times 5280)^2 \times 320.19} = \frac{N}{D} = X$$

Therefore, X = 3,454,100,000,000,000,000 tons. Such then is the magnitude of the attraction between the Sun and the Earth. This force which is in the nature of a stress or tidal action is perpetually at work.

I shall now quote from Mr. Arnold Meyer: [27]"So gradually do we become accustomed to these changes brought about by the tidal forces from day-to-day that they would perhaps escape our notice altogether, so far as the Sun is concerned, were it not for the fact that we are occasionally 'caught out' as it were by the action of the spring tides, which suddenly overflow and flood our public buildings at high tide on the Thames.

"The reason for this is that when the Sun and the Moon are in conjunction they are both concentrating their forces on the same part of the globe at the same time; this, added together, accounts for the abnormal conditions. Under normal conditions, there is always a high tide at London fifty minutes after the Moon has passed the meridian, *i.e.*, tne position the Sun occupies everyday at noon, Greenwich time.

"Since astrology deals more particularly with the effects of heavenly bodies upon *mankind*, it does not require much imagination to appreciate the fact that this conjunction of the Sun and the Moon does definitely affect a child born during conditions of this nature. For within our own bodies, we have innumerable glands whose work is the secretion of hormones. These are for ever adjusting themselves in

27 *Astrology's Place in the World of Science.*

harmony with our chemically changing environment without, and are responsible for our emotions, desires, mental balance, rate of growth, and length of life on this planet."

Mr. Arnold Meyer is fortunately not an 'astrologer' but a scientist and a member of the British Association for the Advancement of Science and author of *The Circulation of Matter, Electrons and Stars*. Therefore we have to attach some weight to his statements.

According to Dr. V Gore, [28]"It is but common-sense to say that the planetary positions of the Sun and the Moon which affect the sea-water causing tides are bound to affect all the store of fluids on the surface of the earth or contained in vegetable kingdom or in human beings.

"The blood is not only a fluid but contains the same salts that are dissolved in the ocean and that too practically in the same proportion. It contains nearly 80% sodium, 4% calcium and 4% potassium. The percentage with respect to magnesium varies. This similarity between the composition of salts in blood and in sea-water is not accidental. Life has its origin in the sea and the earth's early history is one of the sea life and as such it should be susceptible to the same influence of the Moon and the Sun

28 *Astrology, Destiny and Cosmic Factors.*

"Hindu astrologers have given predictions for each day of the lunar month. For the eighth day, that is when the Sun and the Moon are 90° apart they have said *Ashtamayam Vyadhinashastu* or *Ashtami Vyadhi Nashini*. That is the eighth day removes the disease or cures the ailments. On this day the Sun and the Moon, being 90° apart, diminish each other's attractions on the fluids. The blood in the human beings remains thus comparatively in an undisturbed state from the outside influences and any medicine newly started on this day is bound to be more effective if it is properly chosen and that is why there is the importance of this day it being Vyadhinashini.

"Is this not common-sense to use astronomical observations in physiography with respect to physiology and hygiene ? and so if the astrologers claim that transits of planets at a particular time affect the human thoughts or conduct, health and everything that matters then, where is the lie and why astrology should be ridiculed !"

If our activities, physiological and psychological, are regulated by glandular secretions which in their turn are conditioned by chemical changes occurring in nature, then it follows that since the chemical changes are brought about by planetary radiation, man is affected by such electric discharges.

From a gravitational and tidal point of view, the forces of attraction existing between the earth and a few planets are as follows :—

Moon	....	20,185,000,000,000,000 tons
Jupiter	....	138,900,000,000,000 tons
Venus	....	138,250,000,000,000 tons

At a modest estimate, the energy received by the earth from the Sun is about 127,000,000,000,000 h.p. The Sun radiates an incomprehensible amount of energy—nearly 2,200,000,000 times as much energy as that which lights and warms and gives life to our planet and hundreds of millions of times as much energy as is intercepted by all the planets, satellites, etc., combined. In other words, if, the output of solar energy, in terms of units, is 2,200,000,000, then the earth receives only one unit and this infinitesimally small quantity of solar energy shoulders the responsibility of creating, protecting and destroying the entire terrestrial phenomena. Such is the grandeur of the golorious Sun and what wonder the ancients called him *Jagat Chakshu* and *Karmasakshi.*

Thus will be seen the magnitude of arttractions between the earth and the planets is indeed tremendous. This must be continually varying due to the planets continually varying distances from the Sun and from one another. Consequently, the influence of planets upon mankind is undoubted. In a horoscope, the Sun, the Moon and the Lagna represent the soul, the mind and the body respectively of of an individual. The Sun may be visualised as the dispenser of the various cosmic matter, and the Moon as the mixer of this matter, while the Lagna may be taken as a catalytic agent. The other planets are, of course, symbols for interpreting these cosmic influences. How close is our affinity with the Sun, whose chemical elements have spectroscopically been shown not only to be *one and the same* elements as our surroundings here on earth, but actually *indentical* with those found in our own bodies. To put it differently, the ultimate particles of our own body are definitely a part of the Sun itself.

Recent studies of scientists in America and elsewhere have revealed that the sunspots and solar radiations do influence biological behaviour.

Sunspots have been observed over many years and they are found to vary in number with a period whose average length is 11.1 years. Varahamihira had made considerable study of this phenomenon as could be seen from his famous *Brihat Samhita.* Modern authorities conclude as a result of researches that "the existing abnormal changes which we call weather have their origin mainly in the variations of solar radiations". Many places on earth show more rainfall during sunspot maxima than during sunspot minima: Stetson remarks thus: "It is the 23-year period which Dr. Abott believes is particularly important in weather and climate forecasts; the United States is now nearing the close of a period of considerable drought which, according to his best estimate, will not return until the year 1975. He bases his prediction on twice the solar cycle in records of both solar activity and weather. He finds this double period particularly important to precipitation."

We have all heard of ultra-violet and infra-red radiation, etc. Light that is visible to the human eye consists of corpuscles, or perhaps it is wave motion; in any case it is vibrating at different speeds and coming to us in different wavelengths according to that part of the spectrum we choose. [29]"Visible light includes wavelengths of from about 7,700 Angstrom units (abbreviated "A°") which is the limit at the red end, to 3,600 A°, the limit at the violet end. Beyond the red in the spectrum, the long waves are invisible to us but are appreciable as heat waves, and are called the infra-red. If the waves be shorter than 3,600 A°, they are in the region of the *ultra-violet*. However, the human eye varies in range, and some cannot see rays as short as 3,600 A° nor

29 Hugh Rice in *American Astrology*, 1942.

those as long as 7,700 A°. The true ultra-violet comprises waves from 3,600 A° to below 100 A°. The Angstrom is a metric unit of length and is 1/10,000,000 millimetre, a millimetre being about 1/25 inch.

"The Sun contains infra-red, visible and ultra-violet rays, but as to the short-wave side, there is a layer of ozone in the atmosphere, that cuts out all rays shorter than 2,900 A°.

"It is fortunate that most of the ultra-violet light (properly radiation, as 'light' would be visible radiation) is absorbed by the thin layer of ozone in the atmosphere about 25 miles above the surface. For if it were not for the ozone protection, animals and plants would suffer untold harm, unless perhaps they became adapted to the much greater volume of this light. As conditions are, we say that 'just enough' ultra-violet penetrates to help to keep us well and do no real damage. Rays harming the eyes are those shorter than 3,050 A°, those having the greatest value on the skin extend from 2,900 to 3,130 A°, and the beneficial effects are connected with the production of vitamin D. Tanning effects are nature's way of protecting the human race from too much of the ultra-violet radiation because with deepening of skin colour the rays are absorbed and changed to heat rays, and do not penetrate. *Certain of the ultra-violet rays are distinctly bactericidal, notably those form 2,380 to 2,490 A°. These are actually 'death rays' to bacteria."*

The question is, does the ultra-violet content vary with the sunspot cycle? Astronomers have found that it does vary; occasionally as much as 30%. With the increase of sunspots, there is a low point: at least there is a fairly close agreement. We do not infer that the ultra-violet light comes directly from the sunspots but as Stetson says: "It seems entirely possible that such changes as take place in the Sun—that result in its producing more ultra-violet light—so stir up the solar atmosphere that sunspots are naturally concomitant circumstances."

[30]"Plant life is another effect that can be traced to the Sun. Tree rings have been studied for years, especially by Douglass of the University of Arizona. A tree-ring pattern, with its narrow or wide spacing between the rings, indicates the state of the climate during the tree's growth. By this means, weather can be traced back over 3,200 years. Since trees are affected by rainfall or the lack of it, sunspot periods are then related to periods of rain or drought. Where the rings are crowded, a dry season is inferred; similarly where far apart, a season of plentiful rain. Not all investigators agree that tree

30 Hugh Rice in *American Astrology*, 1942.

growth as seen from the rings can be correlated with sunspots, yet based on data of Douglass, it is easily noticed that they do show more growth during years of greatest sunspots.

"The quality of light and its quantity have in the main a three-fold effect on plants: (*a*) the intensity must be right. Chlorophyll, the green pigment, must have enough sunlight to form, but too intense a light is destructive; (*b*) the number of hours per day that a plant is exposed to light partly governs its growth, for defferent plants are sensitive to different lengths of daylight ; (*c*) the wavelength or colour of light has an important effect. Some need rays of the long end of the spectrum in order to grow. It is a complicated matter but some day we shall know much more about it. If the cycle of solar disturbance changes the quality of sunlight very likely the growth of at least some plants is likewise altered ; *quality of sunshine is thought to be really important factor* (italics ours).

"Some good scientists hold that there is nothing at all in the claim that business, manufactures, industry, etc., are all related to solar periodicities ; on the other hand, certain well-known scientists have found a positive correlation. Professor Huntington of Yale, one of the world's leading geographers, believes that solar variations have their results on the health and behaviour of man. Stetson has found that business activity, production of automobiles, building contracts, and other things of this nature have followed sunspots in fluctuations during the last few years. He believes that the hypothesis that sunspots affect business is well on its way to being proved, and that further investigations should confirm the idea."

Readers are aware that the Hindus enjoined certain restrictions in regard to food, etc., a few hours prior to the actual occurrence of an eclipse and during the duration of the eclipse ; for the Moon would screen off corpuscles streaming from the Sun at 100 miles per second and the effect would be some sort of corpuscular shadow and the earth would feel the effect of this corpuscular shadow some two hours prior to the arrival of the 'light shadow'. Recent studies in connection with raido signals reveals a relatively low ionisation density at the time of the corpuscular eclipse, a condition which does not show itself on the day before or on the day after. It is therefore possible that electrical disturbances taking place at times of sunspot activity have some effect on the delicate fibres of our nerves and brain cells, resulting in a change of our temperament and behaviour.

Amongst the villagers in India, it is still an old belief that trees should not be cut near the time of the New Moon for then the sap will dry quickly. That the Moon has an influence on plants has been shown by Dr. L. Kolisko. She has shown through experiments conducted for over nine years that the maximum growth of wheat corresponded with the period of the increasing Moon just after the summer solstice and that "maize was found to grow best when planted two days before Full Moon". Experiments conducted with other vegetables revealed to her a more or less similar correspondence, thus proving the astrological theory of planetary influences on vegetable life.

Gold is always associated with the Sun. In fact one of the names for the Sun is 'Hiranyagarbha'. Dr. Kolisko has even shown the influences of planets on metals. Her experiments were as follows. [31]"A 1% solution of the (metallic) salt or salts to be studied was placed in an open vessel and a cylinder of filter-paper was left standing in it until all the solution had been absorbed by capillary attraction. A 'picture' was thus formed upon the filter-paper which showed that each solution had its characteristic forms and colours. Gold chloride showed consistently the same forms and the same cheerful yellow

31 *Astrology in Everyday Life* by Rupert Gleadow.

colour except during an eclipse of the Sun, when the forms were spoilt and the colour changed to purple."[32]

Physicist Maurice Allen noted at the time of solar eclipse on 2-6-1954 that at the exact moment of the eclipse the pendulum's level of oscillation changed suddenly. His explanation was there must be a cosmic force which the Moon screens from us.

According to Meki Takata of Toho University, Tokyo, the index of floculation of blood suddenly rises when the Sun directs a concentrated beam of waves on earth. Dr. Takata found that during total solar eclipse, as the Moon begins to cover the Sun the floculation index starts to decline reaching its lowest point when the eclipse was complete. Takata concedes, "man is a living sun dial".

That planets influence epidemics is beyond dispute. [33]"Whilst the germ theory about which so much fuss is made by the modern pathologist is an assumption of the causes of the existence of which we have no evidence to account for, the frequency of the coincidence of volcanic eruptions and earthquakes with the outbreaks of epidemics, tends to support the hypothesis of planetary action being

32 For further details reference may be made to Mrs. Kolisko's work *Agriculture of Tomorrow*.

33 *A Text-Book of Astrology* by Dr. A. J. Pearce.

the exciting cause of all these phenomena—the rapid and extreme prostration of muscular strength, a very early symptom, together with excruciating headache, seems to point to electrical changes being intimately associated with influenza and these changes in electrical condition of the atmosphere are due to planetary action."

Professor Tchijevsky has concluded, [34]"that epidemics of influenza have an average period of approximately 11.3 years, which is the same as the sunspot period and among other things that the first wave of a new epidemic of influenza may be expected about three years after every sunspot maximum." His researches enabled him to predict in 1930 the influenza epidemic of 1936. Varahamihira has dealt with the astrological causes for epidemics and plague in his *Brihat Samhita* and this clearly implies some sort of correspondence between certain celestial phenomena and the various types of diseases. It looks as though the investigations of the Russian Professor Tchijevsky, extending over a good many years during which he took into consideration all the important epidemics and plagues since the 15th century have merely confirmed the ancient astrological principles. His conclusions are: (*a*) Epidemics such as influenza have an average

---

34 *Astrology in Everyday Life* by Rupert Gleadow.

period of 11. 3 years—same as the sunspot period. (*b*) The first wave of the epidemic generally occurs about three years after every sunspot maxima. (*c*) And the "virulence of micro-organisms varies in direct relation to the electrical tension of the atmosphere".

Tchijevski has also shown by means of correlation curves remarkable coincidence of sunspot phenomena with the occurrence of revolutions, wars, strikes, agitations, programs against Jews in Russia, lynchings in U.S.A. and population migrations. Dr. Tchijevski has also established an incidence of correlation between sunspot maxima and cardiovascular troubles.

Just like influenza, the peak periods of measles, plague, cholera and other epidemics have also some sort of relation to the sunspots and other periodicities. In reference to the periodicity of measles, we commend the following from [35]Dr. John Brownbe's paper.

"The conclusions which may be based on the results of this investigation cannot in the present state of knowledge be completely formulated. Much more spadework is required before the relative importance of the different factors at work can be accurately gauged. It seems to be proved however

35 *Philosophical Transactions of Royal Society*—208.

that epidemics of measles tend to recur with a regular periodicity which persists often for a long series of years. A great variety in the length of these periods has been found to exist, the shortest period found being that of one year in Paris and the longest that of three years in Dundee, Scotland. Any but a biological explanation of these phenomena seems to be untenable, and the facts further seem to prove that the periodicity is infinitely more probably due to such changes as may easily constitute the life-cycle of an inflicting organism rather than the periodic changes in the susceptibility of the host....It is not unusual for the complete life-history of the measles organisms to *correspond almost exactly with a multiple of the solar year* (italics ours), in itself a suggestive coincidence, but even if this has been duly allowed for, something remains which requires further analysis." Here what interests us most as students of astrology is the *suggested concidence* between the life-history of the measles organism and a multiple of the solar year. The word 'coincidence' is either a cloak to conceal one's ignorance of real facts or a deliberate intention to *ignore* the real cause of a certain phenomenon. When there is a series of coincidences between peak [36]years of deaths from an epidemic and certain variations in solar

36 Walter Bowermann's 'Cyclical Diseases' in *American Astrology*.

energy (which in its turn could only be brought about by variations in the movements of planets with reference to the Sun and themselves), then it can be safely said that some sort of a law exists whereby the next period when the epidemic would recur could be easily anticipated. This is astrology pure and simple.

Students of astrology know that measles, small-pox, etc., are associated with the planet Mars. The tropical year of Mars is 1.88 which is the mean average of its perigee. Whenever Mars makes his closest approach to the earth 'martian epidemics should manifest'. Drs. Faure and Sardou have found out by independent observations that 84% of the passages of sunspots over the meridian of the Sun corresponded to a worsening of their patients. The sunspot maxima corresponds with Jupiter's cycles also because Jupiter goes round the heavens once in about 12 years. This may well suggest that the sunspots are caused by Jupiter's pull as is evident from the periodicity of epidemics. In September 1880, Jupiter was at perihelion (or closest to the Sun); the sunspot maximum in 1883 and 1881 witnessed the maximum of spinal meningitis. Again the same disease reached its maximum in U.S.A. in 1893 (Jupiter at perihelion—July 1892, sunspot maximum 1803): in 1904-5 (Jupiter at perihelion, June 1904—sunspot maximum (1905) and 1917-18 (Jupiter at perihelion in April 1916 and sunspot maximum 1916).

When modern scientists note the coincidence between the sunspot activities during the revolution in France in about 1789, 1830, 1848 and 1870, in Russia in 1906 and 1917, in Spain in 1937 and Hungary in 1956 with mass upheavals, when the increase in corpuscular radiation from the Sun had increased effect on human movements, it looks as though modern astronomers are only confirming Varahamihira of ancient India who had already enunciated this remarkable parallelism between sunspots and earthly affairs—wars, popular uprisings, etc.

Modern meteorology is also noticing a wonderful association between meteorological facts and astrological views. Mr. John, Nelson, Engineer in the RCA Communications Department of U.S.A., has found that what are called the benefic aspects of planets pacifying, apparently, to the ionosphere while other relationships—malefic aspects—disturbing to it. Astrologers predict wars, revolutions and political disturbances when Jupiter, Saturn and Mars are in conjunction, *i.e*, the same degree or mutual angles of 90° and 180° involving certain constellations. Nelson has discovered that the most severe ionospheric disturbances will come when the combined influences of Mars, Venus and Mercury are such that all three will be arranged in positions of great concentration of planetary influence near the Saturn-Jupiter team. And these are correlated to magnetic disturbances on the earth. Naturally, these effects are likely to disturb the delicate and complex systems in the liviug organisms on the earth which regulate and stimulate thought and feeling and action.

When we met Mr. Nelson at a common platform at the "International Astrology Conference" held at New York on 1-5-1971 he said that planets possibly influence the Sun in a manner that caused a temporary change in the Sun's radiation-characteristics although the mechanism of this influence was not known. Mr. Nelson has been able to predict with great accuracy magnetic disturbances based on astrological data.

E. Chapel of Paris, a former General of the French army, pursuing statistical research for more than 30 years, has come to the conclusion that there is a relation between the asteriods, the meteorological conditions and the so-called spontaneous fires and explosions, occurring sometimes by series and for which no rational explanations seem available.

According to Dr. Maurice Faure "everything can be explained in terms of sunspots". Basing his conclusions on the observation of the movements of sunspots from M. Vellot's Observatory at Mount Blanc, Dr. Faure observes: "Out of 25 movements of sunspots 21 were accompanied by significant increase in the incidence of ill-health. Afterwards I established a correlation between movements of the sunspot with successions of sudden deaths."

Dr. Faure is of the view that sunspots are responsible for a whole series of accidents and that the "electric forces emanating from the Sun affect our nervous system and excessive solar activity causes complex effects on man—dejection, attacks of gout or rheumatism, headaches, neuralgia, etc.,"

Traditionally the Sun is associated with vitality and disease of the heart. If the Sun is afflicted in a horoscope it indicates that one is predisposed towards heart trouble. In a letter to the Academy of Medicine dated March 3, 1959, Dr. Poumailloux and M. Viart, Meteorological Engineer, wrote: "Our findings point to a really remarkable correlation between increased frequency of myo-cordial infarctus at certain moments of maximum solar activity and peaks of geomagnetic disturbance."

Dr. Becker, using data available from International Geophysical Year Studies, reveals that patients admitted to hospitals for psychiatric disturbances correlated with solar flares. His research shows that the electrical charge of a person's body changes drastically when the earth's magnetic field is affected. Electrical fields, according to this scientist, are also connected with such physical processes as accidents, would-healing, etc. Seasonal changes in the intensity of geo-magnetic field may explain why susceptibility to various.infections varies with the season.

At an international symposium on relations between solar and terrestrial phenomena, held in Brussels in 1964, Prof. Hellmut Berg of the University of Cologne declared that "serious tubercular cases were in danger of dying on days when there was a violent eruption on the Sun".

Sevente Arrhenius, a Sweedish scientist, proved by statistical investigation, of 25,000 cases, that there is a correlation between the frequency of human births and the revolution of the Moon in the ecliptic.

As a matter of fact, he has shown that menstruation occurs in a large number of women at one particular point in the lunar month. As regards the individual, menstruation usually occurs when the Moon arrives at a certain fixed point in the horoscope Varahamihira clearly mentions in *Brihat Jataka*, that the menses of a woman sets in every month when the Moon is in an Upachaya from the Lagna and that the menses are due to the interaction of Mars and the Moon.

Climate is regulated by the movements and influences of planets. Consequently, the influences of climate are clearly perceptible. If there is any factor in the constitution of man and his temperaments which vitally influences him for work or for laziness, for strength or for debility, for intelligence or for dullness, it is the climate. These instances suggest that between the various atmospherical influences and the vital activity of the human nerves there seems to be a connection which the known sciences have not yet been able to account for, but the effects of which are too often clearly felt to be easily doubted or denied. A change of climate has been firstly considered by the greatest physicians as a most powerful remedy for effecting cures. The seabreeze owes its pre-eminently salutary influences on the health of man to its purity. The extraneous particles which defile the close atmosphere of crowded cities and convert it into a hot bed of diseases and death are mostly absent from the unadulterated air currents which sweep over the wide expanse of water and this fact greatly renders the climate highly salubrious. The moisture tempers the sharpness of the wind, and makes the respiratory organs less liable to the baneful attacks of catarrhal affections. The influence of saline particles, of iodine, of ozone and of peculiar electrical and magnetic conditions, also contribute their beneficial effects.

Dr. Clarence A. Mills, Professor of Experimental Medicine, University of Cincinnati, has found that the contrast between Oriental and Occidental vitality due not to "national, racial or cultural differences, but to climate". "The ebb and flow of human vitality fluctuate with climatic changes, with man's energy rising during stimulation, cold periods, and receding with debilitating calm warmth." When the barometric pressure [37] "is slowly rising, human activity is at its zenith; a medium degree of efficiency occurs when the barometric pressure is at any stable level; and the lowest ebb accompanies falling barometric pressure. Sponge-like, the body and brain cells absorb water and swell when the outside pressure falls. Along with this absorption and swelling there is disturbance of functional efficiency and an upset in the normal body water-balance. On the other hand as the outside pressure rises, the body and brain cells empty and functional efficiency rises". Just before a severe storm, living organismsmanifest increased nervous tension. Animals become bellicose and unmanageable, children tend

37 F. A. Rockwen in *American Astrology*, 1942.

to be peevish and petulent and adults are more irritable and quarrelsome. "There are also obvious physical changes on these low pressure stormy days. As some bodies gain water content their weight increases as much as four or five pounds in one day and there might be some spread of leg or calf circumference. The brain cells cannot expand as they are encased in a rigid structure. Therefore the pressure falls and the resulting intake of moisture from the gastro-intestinal tracts leads to irritability, worry, discomfort and temper flares. In extreme cases if the brain cells become so water-logged that oxygen supply is cut off, fainting or coma may result.

The researches conducted by Dr. Mills of America conclusively prove that climatic conditions influence human growth, vitality, reproductivity, crime, prosperity, health and achievement.

V

ASTROLOGY AND SUPERSTITION

Dr. W. Fliess, a German physician, has studied the annual periodicities in various biological phenomena, thus confirming the persistence of the solar cycle at many places outside the well-known seasonal fluctuations in the rates of marriages, births and deaths. Fliess 'discovered' the cycle of 23 and 28 days as biological data. In one of his publications, he says: "what is most interesting is the fact that the year and the day rule our life just as both of them determine the fast or slow movements of our planets. And that does not involve only our physical but also our spiritual existence, our *creative days* (italics ours)." In other words, almost all Western savants, who have tried to demonstrate the existence of some sort of biological rhythm in human activities, have been indirectly lending support to the astrological theory. According to Gochara or the transit system, the Moon passing through the different signs from his own position in the birth chart is said to make the native's psychological reactions differ on different days. On one day one will be subject to serious fits of depression, on another day to strong sexual urges, on a third to creative thoughts and on the next to fits of illness. All these are discernible astrologically but as long as the scientist looks at astrology through glasses coloured by his own pet theories and prejudiced ideas he has got to be groping in the dark. The following query of Fliess put by himself at the end of his lecture 'Periodical Ways of Man' is germane to the present discussion. "Why wonder? Don't we inherit the physical set-up of our parents, their living substance and consequently ought we not to inherit likewise the characteristics of their substance pertinent to time? This question sets one thinking. Until now we never considered the influence of the year on human existence. That is wrong. For facing the problem created by the year's motion on life, we cannot but expect to find its mark on human beings as well as on the flowering of plants, the mating urge of beasts....Why should it stop at Man? Is not Man a link in the chain of life just as beast and plant are?"

Modern scientific observations have only been corroborating the "superstitious" beliefs held by astrologers that rhythmic occurrences in nature are guided by astronomical influences. What Fleiss, Swoboda and Krafft have observed had been too well known to the ancient Hindus who, having studied the periodicity of psychological and biological functions, have bequeathed to us vast treasures of astrological knowledge. Our ignorance, pride and prejudice come in the way of our appreciating the wisdom of our ancients while we have acquired a knack to nod our heads in approbation if the same principles come out of the mouths of modern scientists. This is indeed a very unhealthy tendency. What we call in the jingle of scientific terminology biological urge', 'psychological impulse' and so on has been explained in simple and easily comprehensible astrological formulae by way of yogas, arishtas and other combinations.

A. N. Whitehead says in his *Introduction to Mathematics* that "the whole life of nature is dominated by the existence of periodic events, *i.e.*, by the existence of successive events so analogous to each other that without any straining of language they may be termed the recurrence of the same event. Our bodily life is essentially periodic. It is dominated by the beatings of the heart and the recurrence of the breathing. The presupposition of periodicity is indeed fundamental from conception of life. We cannot imagine a course of nature in which as events progress, we should unable to say this happened before."

All rhythms in nature, biological or psychological, correspond to cosmical prototypes and are rooted in astronomical relations. From this reason earthly doing and being enlarge themselves to the cosmos and clearly show the unity and harmony in the Universe. And it was just this knowledge that was promulgated by the star lore through ages in that famous formula 'as above, so below.'

A. M. Fox, a Cambridge biologist, brings forward a number of instances by which he proves the existence of lunar periodicities in the living organisms.

H. L. Moore of New York showed the connections between cycles in rainfall and economics and the eight years' periodicity of the planet Venus with respect to the Earth and the Sun.

Similar investigations of many other scientists lead more or less decidedly to the conclusion that a complex relation cannot be denied between certain astronomic periodicities and the occurrence of seisms of volcanic eruptions, of cyclones, as also the variations of other atmospheric pressure, of the growth of trees, etc. "Dr. Budai has collected many other interesting examples of the Moon's influence on human beings. He observes that the day of New and Full Moon, and the two days that precede and follow them are particularly dangerous for health." This is quite in accordance with accepted astrological principles.

On the basis of his findings Dr. Larnord J. Revitz of Duke University has endorsed the ancient belief that there would be more unrest among the insane when the Moon is full: Revitz says: *"Whatever else we may be we are all electric machines. Thus energy reserves may be mobilised by periodic universal factors (such as the forces behind the Moon) which tend to aggravate maladjustments and conflicts already present."

The study of human character and temperament, of endowment and platitudes has become a large department of psychology today. It may surprise many to be told that astrology has a great contribuion to make to this branch of contemporary science

The science and art of the diagnosis of personality traits will be of vital use in many departments of life today—education, industry, administration etc.

The horoscope can construct a fairly accurate picture of the individual's psyche—his temperaments his likes and dislikes, aptitudes, his moods, his abilities and weaknesses and strong traits. For instance it is said that one born when the distance between

* *Psychiatry and Journal of Social Therapy*, July 1966.

the Sun and the Moon is 12° will be 'Vyasanasaktachittascha', meaning 'given to worrying'. This information can usefully supplement the diagnosis of normal psychology arrived at by its vocational tests, its intelligence and other characters of various kinds. It can help educational institutions in guiding students in the choice of careers. It can help industry in making the most of the different types of workers in giving them jobs suitable to thair temperaments. Above all, it can help the individual to guide his plans and career to suit his character traits, avoid lines in which he has no flair and take up lines in which he has a natural aptitude. Astrology reveals the general tendencies inherent in certain types of persons by reason of the positions of the planets and stars at their birth. We can use them in the art of life and make the best of our endowment. Thus one born when Dhanishta and the 8th lunar day coincide will be cruel-hearted, vindictive and easily amenable to sycophancy. If other combinations also indicate rulership, he will most likely become a tyrant, bent on inflicting misery on the people. Other people may beware of such a person and may take suitable steps to neutralise his power for mischief. Or, he himself might try to minimise his evil tendencies by giving them less play in life.

Recent investigations by psychologists have confirmed the diagnostic power of astrology. For instance an American psychologist has made an eightfold classification of human beings corresponding to eight segments of 45° each commencing from the New Moon. According to this classification, whoever is born at any particular phase of the cycle is stamped by the character of that phase. This confirms the ancient idea of the effect of the Moon's affliction in insanity and related diseases.

A French Criminologist has assembled statistics to show that apparently motiveless murders, attacks and criminal behaviour of many kinds rise and fall in a 28-day cycle corresponding to the phase of the Moon. Other observers have noticed similar effects of the Moon on other aspects of life. Dr. Edson Andrews of America has noticed a correspondence between successes and failures in surgery and the phases and positions of the Moon. His record of 1000 cases of tonsillectomy showed 82% bleeding crises occurring between the Moon's first and third quarters. Prof. Ravitz of Pennsylvarian School of Medicine thinks that there is an increase in the electrical potential of human beings every 14 days causing changes of moods—due to the Moon's influence.

The great Swiss Psychiatrist Carl Jung, pupil of Dr. Freud and founder of a variant of psycho-analysis of his own has been a great influence among psychologists and psychatrists to use astrological science in medicine and psychiatry. They have found it illuminating in diagnosing the predispositions of their patients towards certain types of disease, mental and physical. The Moon rules the mind, the Sun rules the soul or self and Mercury rules the nervous system.

The exaggeration of certain traits which occur in normal people as well is caused by a combination of factors involving the Moon, Mercury, the Sun, Mars, etc.

This reminds us of the age-old astrological theory of Hindus.

बुध चन्द्रौ केन्द्रगतौ नान्य ग्रह संयुतौ ।
नपति दृष्ठौं योगेऽयं पैशाचस्तु अत्रं.स्पक्ष स्योन्मादी ॥

meaning that if in a horoscope the Moon and Mercury are in certain mutual dispositions afflicted by Mars, Saturn or the Nodes, it generally indicates mental disorder.

We find such combinations actually occur in the horoscopes of persons suffering from obsessional neurosis, delusions and false views. A false belief is a form of dissociation. When a person in a mental hospital believes that he is the emperor of the world, obviously it is a case of dissociation.

The declination of Mercury can always give a clue as to whether a person will tend to brood over the past, or hug his illusions or escape into a futuristic utopia. But if there is Jupiterian aspect, the picture is entirely changed. The person will be thonghtful and will have much understanding and judgement. Remove the Moon and substitute Mars and you have mechanical aptitude. This is something entirely new in observational science. It is a proven instance of a certain planetary pattern having an effect that the elements of the pattern do not have.

Many psychologists and psychiatrists are experimenting in the U.S.A. and elsewhere with astrological techniques. Many of them (whom I met at New York) are convinced that horoscopes properly cast and intelligently interpreted could be a valuable diagnostic test. They are of the view that "a horoscope is more useful than Rorschach test: A Rorschach shows only the patient's condition at the time of the test whereas a horoscope reveals his basic psychological set-up".

Apart from psychiatry dealing with mental disorder, astrology is of use too in ordinary medicine. This was recognised in ancient India when Ayurveda was linked with Jyotisha, the one practitioner being required to know something of the other. Today this use of astrology is again coming to the force.

An outstanding psychiatrist makes the following observations which must be accepted as justified: "I do not know that somnambulism is more prevalent during the Full Moon, but I know that the sexual organs are more stimulated during this period than at any other time both in beasts and *homo-sapiens*. Seasonal changes, climate, electrical storms and volcanic actions are obviously correlated with the phases of the Sun and the Moon. Every drop of moisture is affected by the Full Moon even as our tides are regulated by it. Menstrual periods are influenced. Moon-struck couples are apt to engage in affairs of the heart during this period. It is the god-mother of *sprooning* couples. Upon the mating instinct of wild and domesticated animals, it has a distinct bearing. At Full Moon hard shells become soft."

The influences of the Moon on human affairs appears with such persistence in the writings of ancient Hindus that it is impossible to ignore their testimony in any orderly survey of the subject. Many of these references rest upon a basis of careful observation and recorded experience. *Bhoutikasutras* observe thus: (1) *Kalakarshanam Suryagolat*, (2) *Suryachandramasou nitya sambandhat*—meaning that the Moon gets its kala or light by attraction from the Sun and that there is interaction between the Sun and the Moon almost every second. Neither the Moon nor the planets are the original sources of light or heat. All receive their light from the glorious Sun. This light is naturally in the shape of vibrations of the light waves. These vibrations are refracted or reflected from the Moon to the earth and vary widely. The vibrations from Mars are much lower and slower than are those from Venus or Mercury and yield a distinction in colour which is perceptible through and measurable by the spectroscope. Vibrations from the Moon also vary greatly in both force and frequency as is indicated by a variation in the Moon's colour from silvery white to ruddy. When we consider that every known basic element emits an individual radiation whose differences are expressed in *Armstrong Units*, it would be strange to presume that these vibrations were without any physical manifestation or influence on earthly matter. The fact is these vibrant rays rouse and move the elements of the earth producing both chemical and physical changes thereof. It is because of these variations in the chemical and physical structure of the earth itself—the base on which all vegetation must be sustained—that the fertility of the soil and the sturdiness of the crop depend in a very large measure upon the Moon. There are many ancient beliefs about the mysterious power of the Moon, many of which science is finding to have a basis in fact. Various ideas once considered superstitious now appear to have some scientific explanations. Based on these observations, the ancient Maharishis have given us a number of combinations which enable us to unravel with appreciable accuracy the amount of *influence* the luna exerts on a particular individual. The ancients have already discovered these effects. All that science has to do is to explain them. You can observe that some lunatics or neurotic people seem to have tides of irrationality rise and fall within them according to the waxing and waning of the Moon. We have personally known a family in which the husband, a short tempered young man, becomes excited as the Moon wanes with the result hardly a New Moon passes without some serious quarrel in his house which upsets his mental equilibrium and renders him uneasy.

All diseases and more especially, skin diseases, insanity and epilepsy were believed to be subject to the influence of the Moon. I should say that here again the ancients were right in their conclusions. We know as a matter of experience that these diseases get more virulent in their effects at the time of the New Moon. No one can deny that.

Whether or not one believes in the influence of the Moon on animal and human organisms, one cannot but be struck with the rhythmic changes in the level of the sea, in atmospheric phenomena and in radio reception keeping step with the Moon's phases. At the time of New Moon or at the time of Full Moon, the tides in the ocean are much greater, the disturbance in the atmosphere more than at other times. Why is this so? Because when the Sun and the Moon are close together in the sky, as at New Moon, or when they are diametrically opposite, as at Full Moon, the two conspire to produce such disturbances; they actually pull at the oceans, draw the water up, as it were in a heap, causing huge tides; they pull at the particles of the gases forming the atmosphere, and if the atmosphere is already disturbed with passing clouds here and there, they supply the spark to produce rain; they pull at you and at me, lifting us all up, so that you would be actually weighing less at New Moon and at Full Moon than at other times. But the greater part of the pull is due to the Moon because of its nearness to us; the Sun in spite of its heavy mass, because of its greater distance, plays only little in the drama. The lifting force due to the Moon is such as to reduce the weight of a body by the fraction $\frac{1}{842440}$ A 4,000-tsn ocean steamer, for instance, loses one pound of its weight when the Moon is directly over head. No measuring instrument has been devised to detect such a minute effect; yet this is sufficient to cause the tides and all the kindred phenomena. Because of the possibility of rain about the time of New Moon when the atmosphere is distrubed, there is a chance for the plants planted at the waxing season to grow better than those planted at the waning. Again as the various cells composing animal organisms respond to the lifting force of the Moon, it is understandable that people suffering from skin diseases, lunacy, epilepsy, diseases involving convulsions and the effects of poisonous bites, suffer more at the time of New Moon than at other times. The sea-urchins because they have their whole being in the waters of the ocean which keep step with the phases of the Moon have their reproductive life regulated by the Moon. I would earnsetly urge physiologists and naturalists to study the correlations between animal life and the phases of the Moon and place their conclusions on a scientific basis.

'We have seen that the solid earth rises and falls under tidal forces and that, as measured by

Michelson, this rise and fall at its greatest is about 9 inches. The rise and fall should be greatest at New Moon, for then the Sun and the Moon together attempt to distort the earth. We know that the earthquake is due to the instability in the earth's crust. It is therefore reasonable to expect this instability to be influenced by tide-producing forces such as result from the Moon's gravitational pull. When the tidal forces are great at the time of the New Moon, they are enough to supply the spark to bring about conditions for an earthquake to happen ; the tidal forces are trigger forces in that they start the mechanism which already is awaiting a spark. It you tabulate the devastating earthquakes of history, you will find that many of them have always occurred about the time of the New Moon. The Great Bihar earthquake occurred on the night of May 31, 1935, a day before the New Moon. Some other earthquakes have occurred about the time of the New Moon when two or more planets were in conjunction. This only strengthens the 'trigger forces' theory; for the gravitational pull of the planets combined with that of the Sun and the Moon tends to create conditions for the occurrence of an earthquake. In spite of much advance of knowledge, the scientist is still unable to predict the occurrence of an earthquake. He is able to predict with great accuracy, years in advance, the occurrence of eclipses and of phenomena far above his head ; but he is helpless in regard to phenomena which occur about him and directly under his feet. Can the astrologer predict the occurrence of earthquakes and thus earn the gratitude of millions living in earthquake areas? Yes, he can provided the ancient principles are carefully studied, properly understood and correctly applied.

VI

STATISTICAL PROOF

That the Moon has a definite effect on the periodicity of human births was demonstrated by a Swiss statistician. K. E. Krafft who based his work on the vital statistics of the canton of Zurich came to the following conclusions. One of the problems essayed by Krafft was that of the similarity of the birth dates, which seem to occur so often among members of the family "These coincidences in which not merely the month, but even the day recur are found too frequently to warrant their attribution to pure chance."[38]

Krafft concluded :[39] (*a*) "that the distribution of female births is much more regular throughout the day than that of male births, (*b*) that about 40 minutes after the Moon has passed to lower meridian the number of births diminishes by 20–50 per cent, but increases again when she reaches a point

---

38 *Astrology in Everyday Life* by Rupert Gleadow.

39 *Ibid.*

60° from the horizon by longitude (this observation was made on a total of 2,218 births), (*c*) that there is marked decrease in births when the Moon is in the second half of the sign Aquarius but when she is in the first ten degrees of Pisces there is a compensating increase, (*d*) that at Full Moon the number of masculine births diminishes and maximum of masculine births is reached about two and a half days after the Full Moon, (*e*) that the number of births increases when the Moon is approaching the ecliptic from the south, and attains a maximum when she is three or four degrees short of her node, (*f*) that male births are more influenced by the Sun, female births by the Moon". Compare these observations of Krafft with the theory of Pranapada propounded by Maharshi Parasara. You will get much food for reflection. According to the sage Parasara, human births can occur only at certain intervals and not always. It is the misfortune of the present century that we hardly think. We advance *a priori* arguments condemning astrology. And we are accustomed to the notion that modern instruments of observation alone can bring to light the nature of phenomena. Objective and inductive study was not a new method in the intellectual life of the ancient Hindus. The methods employed by them to unravel the mysteries surrounding some of the fundamental problems of life are not and cannot be known. It is commonsense to believe that things existed before we were born and that things happened pretty much then as they do now. Still reasonable as belief is, it is not direct knowledge. Even so simple an assertion as 'I was born' involves a distinct succession of deductions with an unquestioning faith in one's postulates. Such an assertion cannot rest on direct knowledge. You may know that you exist; you cannot know so directly that you were born, although the inference is reasonable and the conclusion highly probable. Therefore our pre-possessions should not blind us to the recognition of the simple fact that the astrological theories and combinations were propounded by Sages by methods which are as reliable and trustworthy as those employed by modern thinkers. We should not be under the impression that the conscious substitution of observation and reason for authority and faith as a guide to the realities of the world is a comparatively recent experience.

A French scholar and statistician Michael Gaquelin, who set out to disprove astrology, carried out a rigorous study of astrological matters but soon found substantial ground for accepting that "a specific cosmic seal does affect various physical, chemical and biological reactions". He found "authenticated correlations in a very large number of cases between the positions of the planets Jupiter, Mars, Saturn in the four angles of the horoscope and certain professional types—doctors, military men, painters, priests and Congressmen. Of each category some 500 to 1000 births were considered. He found Mars predominantly in the zones of influence in the horoscopes of men of sports, athletes or officers in the official services. It is together with Jupiter in the charts of generals. Saturn is dominant in the charts of priests. The horoscopes of scientists and medical men reveal Mars, Jupiter and Saturn in zones of activation".

In the words of Dr. Gaquelin : "In other words, we somehow had to integrate our peculiar planetary effects into the total picture of modern science. The problem was, how could this be done ? One possibility is that some form of radiation issuing from the planets marks the newborn at birth with an influence whose effect persists the whole life long. Let us take an example : If a child is born when Mars is rising. We could assume that the planet exerts sudden action that modifies the child's organism. After this action, the child would have 'something more' than his parents gave him through heredity. And this 'something more' would have sufficiently strong and lasting influences to result in the child's having specific gifts and a definite orientation toward his existence." But Gaquelin's investigations are confined to Western concepts. His ideas about Hindu astrology are perverse and prejudiced.

The French mathematician Paul Choisnaurd investigated the horoscopes of 119 persons of great intellectuals. His investigations revealed that in none of these cases, the Moon was to be found in the sign of Scorpio. "Theoretically his study is open to this objection that intellectual power is a matter of opinion and appreciation rather than fact." But in reality his list was composed of all those persons who had attained great distinction in Philosophy, Science, etc., such as Flammarian, Byron and others. [40]"And yet, of 1,450 ordinary people 140 were found to have the Moon in Scorpio. This extraordinary deviation from the laws of probability may surprise any one but an astrologer; yet is quite in harmony with astrological principles which say that the Moon in Scorpio gives strong feelings, and intensely personal outlook and violent prejudices. Thus placed, the Moon evidently hinders the development of the candour and fair-mindedness that characterise the greatest intellects.' According to astrological rules, Mars is the military

40 *Astrology in Everyday Life* by Rupert Gleadow.

planet. If astrology is true, then horoscopes of all military leaders must have Mars strongly disposed. In 200 horoscopes of military men 'taken at random,' Choisnaurd "found that Mars had considerably more aspects among the soldiers"—Here is the table he drew up showing the percentage of each class who had Mars in aspect to any given planet :

Mars in aspect to	*Percentage of civilians*	*Percentage of soldiers*	*Margin*
Mercury	44	58	*plus* 14 per cent
Venus	36	50	" 14 "
Uranus	45	58	" 13 "
Sun	50	60	" 10 "
Moon	50	60	" 10 "
Jupiter	54	59	" 5 "
Saturn	45	50	" 5 "
Neptune	46	48	" 2 "

Prof. Ellsworth Huntington in his *Main Springs of Civilisation* deals exhaustively with cycles and has some interesting information to give that could be considered to have a bearing upon astrological theories. Some of his conclusions are : (1) Conceptions normally are more numerous in June as something happens to us then biologically, (2) births of world prominent people happen in February,

(3) occurrence of suicide, insanity and sex crimes reach a maximum in July and August, (4) there is seasonal variation in mental activity also. He has also detected the existence of rhythms in intellectual activities, emotional disturbances and the like. Prof. Wesley Mitchell says that in business no other cycle is as strong as that of 41 to 43 months. If the ancient Hindus had no knowledge of these rhythms, *i.e.*, correspondences between celestial configurations and terrestrial developments, how could they have given rules whereby the future trend of commercial events could be anticipated ? For instance, we are told in an ancient astrological work that whenever Mars enters Leo, gold, copper and all red-coloured articles would become available in plenty with the result, there will be increased business activities pertaining to these metals. Mars enters Leo once in 540 days. This is an important cycle whose effects, when carefully studied, may reveal facts of great importance to the commercial world.

If astrology be true it follows that any two people born on the same day at the same place, and at same hour, will have a similar destiny. K. E. Krafft has shown this to be true.

[41]"In his book *astro-physiologic* published at

41 *Astrology in Everyday Life* by Rupert Gleadow.

Leipzig in 1928 Krafft drew up a list of 72 persons of 2 or 3 who were born approximately the same hour, day and place, and invariably, they have died at about the same age and in a similar manner. The data were obtained from civil registers of the towns of Basle and Geneva and it is open to any one to verify them. We cannot quote the whole list but a few examples are given. Coincidence might explain a single case. But an unbroken series of thirty coincidences must surely be a little too much for any one's credulity."

In this connection, we should not forget to recognise the labours of some of the Western astrologers who have shown statistically the truth of astrology. Symours considering the horoscopes of over one hundred centenarians came to the following conclusion: [42]"Aries and Leo are particularly frequent as rising sign, but the signs of earth, particularly Virgo, are rare. The eighth house is far more rarely occupied by planets than any other. The Sun and the Moon have hardly a single square of Saturn and Mars," but plenty of good aspects from Jupiter and Venus. Our own researches to which we shall subsequently make a reference reveal convincing results.

Whether we call it deterministic principle, karmaic indication or planetary influence, the fact

---

42 *Astrology in Everyday Life* by Rupert Gleadow.

is that the existence of correlations between celestial changes and terrestrial phenomena is demonstrated. We do not know and we cannot know whether living organisms show the same rhythms as the heavenly bodies, but we know for certain that they exhibit analogous periodicity. The precession of the equinox in the different constellations seems to be intimately related to the different phases of human culture. Astrology, it seems to us, can help to solve the mysteries of evolution. It provides such a frame of reference that human evolution can be seen in a truer perspective and with greater objectivity. The zodiac is a measuring rod. For instance, the axis of the earth is supposed to take a period of about 2,592,000 years to make one complete turn. We may suggest that during each one of these revolutions one of the main phylogenetic divisions of humanity may have been produced. The Negro, Mongolian and Caucasian races of the present day represent the last three waves of evolution according to this scheme, but it allows more time for man's evolution than palaeontologists are disposed to admit. Enough is said about these periodicities in the articles that have appeared in THE ASTROLOGICAL MAGAZINE that it would be unnecessary to quote them here.

Place of Birth	*Number in Civil Register*	*Sex*	*Date and Hour of Birth*	*Date of Death*	*Cause of Death*
Plainpalais	1	F	22nd Jan. 1822 9 a.m.	26th June 1906	Senile Decay
Geneva	39	F	22nd Jan. 1822 10 a.m.	17th Jan. 1908	Do.
Geneva	273	F	22nd May 1833 1 a.m.	24th Apr. 1920	Bronchial Inflamma-ation
Versoix	11	F	22nd May 1833 2 a.m.	1st Jan. 1921	Do.
Basle	2648	F	18th Sep. 1901 3-30 a m.	5th Sep. 1920	Flu and Meningitis
Basle	2656	F	18th Sep. 1901 4-20 a.m.	30th Apr. 1919	Flu and Tuberculosis
Basle	2194	F	7th Aug. 1901 9 a.m.	1st Jan. 1921	Pulmonary Tuber-culosis
Basle	2195	M	7th Aug. 1904 9 a.m.	31st May 1919	Do.
Geneva	229	F	8th Aug. 1904 7 a.m.	20th Feb. 1921	Do.
Geneva	47	M	18th Feb. 1901 2-45 a.m.	11th Feb 1921	Asphyxiation by carbon monoxide
Near Geneva	88	M	18th Feb. 1900 3 a.m.	22nd May 1909	Asphyxiation by drowning
Basle	498	M	18th Feb. 1901 4 a.m. amniotic liquid	18th Feb 1901	Asphyxiation by inhaling amniotic liquid

The facts so far adduced show clearly that man is subject to cosmic influences. As ultra-violet and infra-red rays and other electrical wavelengths readily penetrate the human body and even the solid bone of the ordinary person's head, so it is evident that these excess rays primarily affect emotional, mental and psychical faculties probably through the glandular system. It is apparent therefore that we are living in a veritable sea of vibratory energies which silently, unerringly and equitably supply the means of creating, maintaining and destroying the myriads of forms of life in our little universe, according to the response of each to the different stimulations and according to capacity and needs of each at their stage of evolution. A dog under prolonged irritation of excess or ultra-violet or infra-red rays may go mad and bite people. A human being might control and direct the increase of energy into powerful efforts towards bettering his own conditions.

I have with me fifty horoscopes of persons who have died from tuberculosis. The Ascendant or the Lagna is hardly Aries, Leo or Sagittarius. Malefic planets were invariably found in Gemini and Virgo and Jupiter and Venus were highly afflicted.

The law of heredity is equally felt in the astrological maps of families, by repetition of common astrological factors. What we call 'Rajayogas' are certain special dispositions of planets affecting the combined radiation at the particular moment of birth in such a way that the native would become great, famous and outstanding. The moment of birth is not certainly an insignificant epoch. The child about to issue out of the womb will be in a plastic state and the delicate glandular organisms are readily moulded by the planetary influences surrounding us. Every thing depends upon the *precious minute* or Muhurtha when all the glands of the body are adjusted and nature fixes her seal. Strange as it may seem, the mixing of various ingredients caused by the interaction (or chemical affinity) of the different planets with the matter of our own body at the time of one's birth definitely portray one's character and therefore destiny.

Some people suggest that the truth of astrology must be "demonstrated" as if in astrology we merely handle material objects. But if the truth (or falsehood) of astrology is to be demonstrated, it does seem to us necessary to ask, first, what constitutes demonstration.

Astrology purports to describe the character and destiny of persons. So does history. History is surely a discipline of unchallengeable reality. But is it science? And is demonstration, in the strictest sense of that term, possible within history? Was Aurangzeb a good or a bad man? Was Mary Queen of Scotts a good or a bad woman? That is a very human question, as also a very legitimate historical question which admits of precise historical treatment. But does the answer, one way or another, admit of "scientific" demonstration? Can you put it "to an impartial test"?

Those of us who might wish to affirm the goodness of the Scottish Queen often find ourselves in very great perplexity. Yet that Mary Stuart was defeated at Langside, that she was a less able politician than Elizabeth or Cecil, that she was executed at Foitheringay are historical facts, and are certainly not scientific facts and they do not admit of scientific demonstration. They admit of the kind of demonstration that is possible within history. But that does not mean that there is anything vague or indeterminate about them. Now astrology has at least this much in common with history: that part—at least—of its aim is to portray human character. But it differs from history in so far as part—at all events—of astrology has also reference to scientific facts. In so far as astrology relates to facts of the scientific order, it does admit of scientific demonstration. And scientific demonstration ought to be given and has--in actuality—been given.

That the higher reaches of astrology are concerned with human character and human experience necessarily places astrological truth outside the possibility of "scientific demonstration", just as, for example, the "truth" of portrait painting or of historical portraiture also lies outside that possibility. Yet alike astrological, historical and artistic portraiture are subject each to its own proper kind of critical judgment. It requires genius, however—of something akin to that—paint a portrait of whose artistic truth it is worthwhile speaking. It also requires genius—or, at least, a quite specific astrological gift—to achieve the parallel task within the astrological field. Where is that astrological genius or talent—to be found, and who is to recognise it if it were found? Certainly not the scientifically trained mind. It is just not the scientist who is capable of passing any sort of discerning judgment about astrology. That is the radical mistake of those who ask for a 'demonstration of astrology'. It is not at the bar of science that astrology in its very nature can stand or fall. The historian, the psychologist, the poet, the novelist might have some astrological discernment. The scientist as such could have none.

Render unto Caesar the things that are Caesar's. Therefore, the dubious critics of astrology should begin by consideration of those branches of astrology that refer to the objective world only and not to experience. Let them first scrutinise such work as Krafft's and then perhaps they will be aware of the difficulty contained in the question how one passes from the knowledge of the world of external objects to the knowledge of the world of inner experience.

It is a remarkable thing that the important events of life always happen at astrologically important moments, that is to say, when the Dasas and Bhukthis (astrological time-measures) of powerful or weak planets operate. As an example, we can take up the horoscopes of Napoleon, Hitler, Mussolini, King George VI, Hirohito and Stalin. The dominant combinations in Hitler's horoscope are the disposition of Saturn in the 10th and Mars in the 7th, each aspecting the other powerfully. Jupiter the benefic is however consigned to a minor position. Astrological text-books say that Mars and Saturn combination (which includes aspects also) in certain houses, subject, of course, to the general strength or otherwise of the horoscope is said to make the subject extremely aggressive. It is not mere coincidence that this disposition of planets obtains in the Fuehrer's horoscope. A warning was given in THE ASTROLOGICAL MAGAZINE, as early as 1937, in the following words :—

"The nativities of Mussolini and Hitler will drift Europe towards a dangerous zone. It now remains for countries with wiser statesmen to set right the equilibrium in European politics. Note the Emperor of Japan's horoscope and see how Italy, Germany and Japan with absolute impunity break the public law of the world." As regards the fates of Hitler and Mussolini enough had been written by us in the columns of THE ASTROLOGICAL MAGAZINE. The following extracts will show how predictive astrology reveals the future in a remarkable manner:

[43]"The second part of the Moon's sub-period commences from about 11th October 1944 and continues for nine months. It is only during this period that Hitler's career must come to an end. Developments in Germany in the near future will be sudden, dramatic and unexpected and Hitler would have a violent end especially because of the powerful disposition of Mars."

The above delineation is one that will commend itself to the student of astrology, particularly the position of Mars referred to in the last line, it being

---

43 THE ASTROLOGICAL MAGAZINE, 1943 issue.

a common observation that Mars in the house of death signifies a violent end. In Hitler's case, the Sun is in deep exaltation in the 10th degree of Aries. When he was sent to prison at the end of March 1924, Saturn was exactly in the opposite degree (Lagna). In regard to Mussolini and Italy, the following forecast may be noted with interest :

[44]"1943 and 1944 loom as important years for Italy foreshadowing the destruction of Fascism. Storms are also brewing in the horoscope of Prince of Piedmont and will break when he ascends the throne. Saturn by transit passes through the orb of this degree by about October 1944 and the exact degree is transited by about July 1945. Thus about this time something tragic may happen to the Duce."

Mr. Cyril Fagan, writing in March 1955 issue of *American Astrology* of New York, observes thus :

"In April 1947 issue of THE ASTROLOGICAL MAGAZINE, the Editor Dr. B. V. Raman made one of the most successful predictions of modern times, when he penned these words : 'Mars and Saturn will be in conjunction in the last degree of Cancer on November 12, 1947. These combinations also point to the loss (by assassination as violent Mars is with Saturn in the 12th) of a respected mass leader of this country' (p. 247). There cannot be the slightest

44 THE ASTROLOGICAL MAGAZINE, July 1943 issue.

doubt but that Dr. Raman had Gandhi's Rasi Chakra before him when he wrote these ominous words, for the conjunction of Mars and Saturn, to which he refers, occurred at 11h. 21m. 45s. U.T. on November 12, 1947, when the sidereal longitude of the malefics was Cancer 28° 06′ 28″ and therefore close to Gandhi's Moon in Cancer 26° 55′. Gandhi was assassinated at New Delhi on January 30, 1948 (see horary chart) so that Dr. Raman's prediction, which was published at least 10 months before the event, found an astonishingly accurate, if tragic, fulfilment. The confirmation of this forecast puts Dr. Raman in the foremost rank of the world's successful astrologers and renders the study of Jyotisha really worthwhile."

The above are the astrological predictions, pure and simple, made quite in advance and based upon astrological principles. The introduction of this personal element in an essay on astrology is to be deplored but since proof is needed to convince the sceptic, such a digression may be ignored by the indulgent reader.

It is a common knowledge that the tenth house or the meridian is a conspicuous position in a horoscope and it is said to rule one's means of livelihood and public career. Saturn in (or aspecting) the 9th and 10th is always supposed ultimately to indicate fall from high position. The horoscopes of Phillip II of Spain, Napoleon I, Louis XVIII, Kaiser, Hitler and Mussolini are illustrations of the dominance of Saturn whilst Jupiter extremely well placed has given quite the opposite results in respect of Elizabeth I, George III, Queen Victoria, George V and George VI.

VII

ASTROLOGY AND HISTORY

The relation between astrological facts and great political events in human history opens up a vast field of fertile and illuminating study. History and astrology will throw light on each other and may offer valuable guidance to statesmen. The transits of Saturn through Aries for instance show frequent and astonishing coincidence with great events in English history. When Saturn was in Aries in 1939 England had to declare war against Germany.

Similarly in Indian history, the transits of Saturn in Cancer and Jupiter in Pisces seem to have important consequences. When Saturn was last in Cancer, three important events took place in India: the Independence of India, the birth of Pakistan and the death of Mahatma Gandhi. Calculating backward, we have the series of events: the first battle of Panipat, second battle of Panipat, first Mysore War, first war of Independence, etc. The birth of the Indian National Congress and Montague's declaration of Responsible Government have all happened while Saturn was in Cancer. If the two series—Saturn in Cancer and Jupiter in Pisces—happen to intersect each other, we should expect events of great importance to occur. This series fell in 1857–1858 when the first War of Independence was waged, and it fell again in 1975-76 when emergency was declared and an authoritarian regime established. This proved to be a very significant period in Indian History. Outstanding predictions, such as Nixon's fall from power in 1975, developments in Iran leading to the exit of the Shah, recent affairs in India, earthquakes in Iran, developments in S. Africa made in the columns of THE ASTROLOGICAL MAGAZINE have all been fulfilled.

There seem to be enough basis for the study of what may be called *political astrology*. I venture to say, risking derision by those in control of National Governments that a competent astrological bureau could give Government enough insight into future complications with foreign powers that would be worth millions of rupees, even if only 60% of its predictions come out true.

Astrologers have also found a 20-year periodicity in the correlation between the deaths of American Presidents in office and Jupiter–Saturn conjunctions.

1840—W. H. Harrison, elected President, died in office from an assassin's bullet.

1860—Abraham Lincoln, elected President, was assassinated.

1880—James A. Garfield, elected President, was shot to death.

1900—William Mackinley elected President for a second term and died later during his term of office.

1920—Warren C. Harding elected President and died in the White House.

1940—Franklin Roosevelt elected President to a third term and died in office.

1960—Kennedy elected President and was shot dead in office.

The late Prof. B. Suryanarain Rao has quite a number of remarkably correct predictions to his credit. Analysing the Lunar Year Ananda (1914-15) he observed thus in the March 1914 issue of THE ASTROLOGICAL MAGAZINE :

"There will be sudden outbreaks of passion and excitement among the armies leading to anarchy and denunciation of old kingly authority, great loss and consternation and the war fever will be at its highest pitch. A European war is threatened.......... and the United States should be very careful in not being dragged into a ruinous war. Two deaths among the European royalties are indicated and one of them will be from violence or treachery. Political relations all over the world during the months of August and September will be highly excited on account of the solar and lunar eclipses following one after the other within a fortnight."

The assassination of the Arch Duke of Austria and the outbreak of the first world war are all matters of history and need no exposition.

According to Tehijevsky, in England the Liberals are said to have been in power during sunspot peaks and the conservatives when the sunspots were scarce.

Late R.A. Proctor, a great astronomer, repeatedly delighted himself in attacking this 'hoary' and "exploded superstition to which, however, he conceded a noble past, historically, and a perfectly reasonable basis in theory. But he went on to add, "this fascinating theory which has in every age attracted the greatest minds does not work out in practice and hard fact". A careful study of all that Mr. Proctor has written on the subject shows conclusively by the ludicrous blunder made, that he had not acquired enough practical knowledge of the science to even cast a horoscope and much less to interpret the same. Once he ventured out of the forest of generalities into the open to challenge the enemy (Astrology) and fell a victim to his temerity. In the

Cornhill Magazine for July 1877, appeared an essay from his pen entitled "The Planet of War" in which the following passage occurs :—

"But if Mars were in truth the planet of war, if his influence poured from near at hand (in perigee) upon the nations of this earth, excited them to war and bloodshed, we might well fear that coming months would bring desolation in many fair terrestrial fields. For Mars has not blazed so fiercely in our skies since 1845, nor will he so shine again for 47 years."

[45]"The God of War, who has an occasional rough sense of humour, did pick up the gauntlet thus contemptuously thrown at him. The Russo-Turkish War, declared on 24-4-1877, and first regarded by European diplomacy as a mere 'walk-over' for the Russians, soon developed symptoms of unexpected severity. On the very day on which Mars entered his domal dignity Aries, Plevna was carried by storm with a carnage unsurpassed in history. The last Napoleonic Wars (and the 1st and the 2nd World Wars) should all be construed as ironical answers of planets to the pedants who dare to dispute their influences on the destinies of mankind."

[46]"Sir John Herschel eharacterised the assertion

---

45 *A Text-Book af Astrology* by Dr. A. J. Pearce.

46 Ibid.

that comets cause 'warm summers, epidemics and so forth' as 'all wild talking.' History however abounds with coincidences of epidemics, wars, overthrow of kingdoms, famines and earthquakes with the appearance of great comets. Hence by an empirical law we may venture to say when a great comet, or several, shall appear, certain great events will immediately follow. But this would by no means necessarily involve a belief that the comets were the *cause* of such events, for all these phenomena might be the result of a common natural cause." Shakespeare must have intuitively realised the significance of the appearance of comets in the following lines :—

> When beggars die there are no comets seen ;
> The heavens themselves blaze forth the death of princes.

Varahamihira has dealt with the question of comets in his *Brihat Samhita*. He uses the term Kethu for these occasional visitors. The effects generally depend upon their positions in the particular zodiacal signs. The list of *coincidences* furnished below must convince any fair-minded critic that after all the appearance of comets is not merely of scientific (?) interest but indicates something else also.

Daniel Defoe in his *Journal of the Plague Year* mentions how much the alarm in London was increased, when the great plague of the year 1665 was in its early stages, because a blazing comet had appeared some weeks earlier. This comet was of a "dull languid color" and its motion, "very heavy, solemn and slow", the interpretation being that "a heavy judgment, slow but severe, terrible and frightful was already begun. In 1666 a little before the Great Fire, another comet appeared, portending a judgment "sudden, swift and fiery". He mentions that many remarked "that those two comets passed directly over the city, and so very near the houses that it was plain they imported something peculiar to the city alone".

In August 1193 B.C. there appeared in Gemini a comet of most dreadful aspect, visible throughout Egypt, and immediately followed by the death of King Amenemas. In 479 B.C. a comet was observed by the Grecians, which was crooked like a horn and lasted twenty-two days. During this time occurred the sea fights at Salamis. In 430 B.C. a fiery and red comet hung over Athens for seventy-five days, and the Pelaponnesian War began. In 371 B.C. there was a great comet like a beam, extending over 60 degrees of the horizon. This was at the time of the inundation and earthquake in Achaia. In 356 B.C. at the birth of Alexander the Great, appeared a comet at first bushy and bearded, which afterwards took the form of a spear. In 134 B.C. at the birth of Mithridates, King of Pontus, a comet was visible of extraordinary size and splendour. In 183 B.C. a comet in Pisces, bright as the Sun, was coincident with the death of Scipio Africanus, and again at the death of Caesar. In 71 A.D. there appeared a great comet in Virgo, the ruler of Jerusalem. This comet took the form of a sword directly over that city. This occurred on Easter Sunday, the 8th of April. It was visible a whole year, until the taking of this city by Titus. In 218 A.D. a great comet was visible in Pisces eighteen days, during which time Heliogabalus defeated Macrimus and became Emperor of Rome. In 323 A.D. a comet in Virgo appeared coincident with Constantine's victory over Lucinius and in 337 A.D. another comet in Aries, of terrible grandeur, was simultaneous with the death of Constantine. In 392 A.D. a small, bright comet appeared in the heavens above Rome. The same night Valentinian, the Emperor, was strangled in his place. In 493 A.D. there was a great comet in Virgo ; for when Rome was sacked by the Goths under Alarac on two previous invasions in 396 and 402 A.D. a comet appeared like a sword. In 423 A.D. there appeared a terrible comet which foretold the war between Rome and Persians. In 455 A.D. Rome was sacked by Genseric when a great comet appeared. In December 539 A.D. a large comet appeared in Sagittarius, which remained about forty days during which nearly three lacs of people perished by the earthquake at Antioch. In 546 A.D. a comet, in the shape of a lance, was visible over the city of Constantinople, and during the time that it remained ten thousand persons died daily of the plague. In 570 A.D. a comet appeared when Italy was taken by the Lombards. In September 602 A.D. a comet, in the shape of a sword, hung over Constantinople, and the execution of the Emperor Maurice followed. In May 604 A.D. a bright comet was visible at Rome and Gregory the great died. In 613 A.D. a fiery comet, visible over a month, hovered over Rome and the Persian War began. In 800 A.D. a large but mild and beneficent comet was visible with the transfer of Empire of Charle-magne, and another in November of 814 A.D. was immediately followed by his death. In the year 1106 A.D. a comet was seen in the east, sending beams, like burning torches and fiery darts. This marked the beginning of the terrible wars of Crusades. In July 1264 A.D. appeared in Taurus, a comet of most signal magnitude. This remained three months and disappeared the night Pope Urban the fourth died. The comet of 1456 June (supposed to be Hally's comet) saw the surrender of Constantinople to the Turks. The next appearance of Hally's comet in 1531 was followed by the raging of spotted fever all over Europe and by the death of over 30,000 people in the famous Lisban earthquake. When the same Hally's comet reappeared in 1682, Catana was destroyed by an earthquake and 60,000 died. Then in 1759 the same comet was visible, followed by outbreak of earthquakes in Tripoli, Syria, etc. In 1909, the death of Edward VII followed the appearance of the same comet. Coming to modern times, there are any number of instances demonstrating the fact that the appearance of comets has been followed by great calamities, the most recent one being the death of Mahatma Gandhi soon after the appearance of a comet.

It may not be out of place to mention here that whilst most of the predictions made by real astrologers have turned out to be correct, the world was alarmed several times by the predictions of learned astronomers. In 1856, great excitement was caused by the prediction of a learned astronomer that the comet of 1556 would re-appear and come into collision with the earth. Many persons went foolishly mad about the comet which after all never appeared.

Prof. Corrigan, Director of Carlton University, once stated in an article in *Popular Astronomy* that "the certain destruction of the world is imminent through the breaking away of a new planet from the Sun, producing a terrific explosion which will probably smash the earth and surely destroy all animal life on land as well as in waters". The professor was a clever man, more shrewd than astrologers. While his calculations based on mathematics gave him informationr egarding the particular time of detachment of the planet from the Sun, they did not reveal to him the possible date, on which the catastrophe would occur. Dr. Falbe of Austria fixed definitely the end of the world on 13th November 1899 at 3-3 p.m. We are now in beginning of 1982 and thank God, Dr. Falbe's prophecy has been falsified. Lord Kelvin was of course more guarded. He did not bind himself to any date on which the world would be destroyed. He fixed about four centuries for the destruction of all living beings on the surface of the earth for want of oxygen as this precious "a something will all have been consumed by that time by men and industrial workshops. There was again another panic creator in the shape of Mr. Gore of the Royal Astronomical Society. Mr. Gore observed thus about the speedy destruction of the world: "The Sun is about to collide with one of the spent stars that loom darkly in space. In about 11.8 years the distance would be reduced to 4,000 millions, and in about 14 years the dark body would reach the orbit of Uranus or rather it would be at the same distance

9

from us as Uranus for its path will not intersect the orbit of the planet. Both planets would be reduced to gaseous state within an hour and a stupendous amount of heat will be produced sufficient not only to destroy the earth but most of the planets of the solar system. In THE ASTROLOGICAL MAGAZINE for December 1898, a year before Dr. Falbe's time fixed for destruction of the world, in the issue for May 1906, a couple of years before the time fixed by Mr. Gore, Prof. Rao wrote strongly against these panic mongers and assured the public that no heed be given to the predictions of these erratic scientists.

Another wise Solomon (of course astronomer) came forward with startling predictions that between 17th and 20th December 1919, tremendous things were going to happen. To quote this prediction in full of Professor Albert Porter, would cause unnecessary pressure on pages of this book. He went so far as to say 'that the whole solar system would be strongly out of balance on account of the conjunction of six planets which would pull jointly on the Sun. Even then Prof. Rao came to the rescue of the people to drive out panic, when he strongly asserted in THE ASTROLOGICAL MAGAZINE for October 1919 that no combinations were available according to Hindu calculations, which would disturb the equilibrium of the solar system. Prof. Rao observed:

"What does the idiotic professor mean that on that day six mighty planets are within 26 degrees of each other?" He further continued thus: "We assure the people that no such cataclysms happen and they may quietly attend to their work."

"Had an astrologer foretold such calamities" observes Dr. Pearce, "the newspapers would have viewed with virtuous indignation and denouncement when the scare was found to be groundless. This fiasco is not remembered against astronomers, and this marks the difference between orthodox and heterodox science."

Astronomers claim to have discovered a singular bond of relationship between comets and shooting stars. But hitherto they have failed to determine either the origin, the real structure, or the causes of the wonderful changes of shape of comets.

Dr. Richard Garnett, Editor of the famous *Encyclopaedia of Literature* series is of opinion that astrology with the single exception of astronomy is, as regards data, the most exact of all exact sciences.... Some of his other observations are: "The principles of his (astrologer's) art have come down to him in essentials from the most remote antiquity, they have been published in a thousand books and are open to the examination of all the world. His calculations are performed by no more cabalistical process than arithmetic. It is the peculiar boast of his system, in its application to human beings, to enthrone law where law would be otherwise unrecognised and to leave no opening for anything preternatural." In his article 'The Soul and the Stars' published in the *London University Magazine* for 1880, he adduces the examples of such historical personages as Emperor Paul, George III, Gustavus IV, Empress Charloin, Charles II of Spain and a host of other insane monarchs and ably shows how mental diseases are liable to occur to when Mars and Saturn occupy certain positions in the horoscope. He also gives examples of what he calls 'eccentricity accompanied with great mental power', the horoscopes considered being those of Voltaire, Feebre, Archbishop Whately, Gladstone and Saint Simon, in all of which he finds a certain juxtaposition of Mercury with Mars and Uranus, and concludes his famous essay with the following words : "We claim nothing more than to have established a *prima facie* case, and to have earned the liberty of speculating against. Such speculations carried to their legitimate consequences would produce a more momentous revolution in human thought than all the discoveries of this wonderful age." Richard Garnett was no astrologer. He was a Curator of the British Museum and has studied many fields of science. Therefore his deductions merit the serious consideration of all critics of astrology.

In astrology, Venus is supposed to rule marriage and the sex element. His presence in the 7th excites passions and the person will be highly sexed. Mars in combination with Venus indicates more than one marriage, want of happiness from marriage, etc. This is strikingly brought out in almost every horoscope examined by us in which Mars–Venus affliction is present. Out of sixty horoscopes studied by us containing Mars–Venus combination, 18 cases of violent quarrel and separation are to be found when Mars and Venus were in exact conjunction in the 2nd house. In 40 cases more than one marriage had taken place. In the two remaining cases, no abnormality could be seen. No high intelligence is necessary to appreciate the simple truth that in the majority of cases of melancholia Saturn will be dominant.

The association of Venus with Saturn, Mars or Rahu is always indicative of either want of happiness in domestic life or oversexuality making one seek illegal sex gratifications. Though I do not wish to burden the indulgent reader with astrological technicalities, I must commend to his attention the following two horoscopes out of the several hundreds in my collection, typically illustrative of certain astrological dicta :

In Chart No. 1, Venus is associated with Rahu while two malefic planets are to be found on either side of this combination. The subject's wife was always sickly—until her death. He did not actually

		Sun Moon	Venus Rahu
Mercury Jupiter			Mars
	Chart No 1		
Ascdt.			

	Moon Ascdt.		
Sat			
	Chart No. 2		
	Sun Mercury Rahu	Mars Venus	

marry a second wife but had his own immoral ways. He suffered from venereal complaints and had absolutely no peace of mind. In the other chart, there is again a conjunction of Mars and Venus. The Moon and Mercury, rulers of the mind, are subject to aspect and association respectively of Saturn, and the Sun and Rahu. The man married twice. He had a terrible turn of venereal mind and contacted severe forms of female diseases from which he suffered a great deal. His two wives died before him. He had absolutely no family happiness. Instances can be multiplied to show that a certain juxtaposition of Venus, Mars and Saturn always gives rise to sexual aberrations and marital inharmony. If such afflictions are present in the horoscopes of children, they *indicate* the trend of the mental development and by bringing up the children in a strict, moral and religious atmosphere, they could be made fitting citizens.

[47]The birth of twins and their differing lives are sometimes produced as an argument against astrology. When the question of twins is rightly understood, the argument will really be in favour of astrology. Twins are sometimes alike and sometimes different. Sometimes twins will have some common character and others different. Such variations as a rule are due to slight difference in the time of birth. The word twin implies two entities coming into manifestation under the same planetary pattern. This must also be extended to include two children born approximately (if not exactly) for the same time regardless of parentage or environmental conditions of birth. Many curious cases in point have come to our attention. In fact, I have with me the horoscopes of two other persons born on the same day

---

47 *Gleadow*.

that I was but at different times. One is a doctor, the other is a banker and what the third is, the reader knows. The remarkable fact is that in all the two other cases some of the important past experiences have paralleled those of mine. On 16th February 1937, an international news from Detroit announced the discovery of two seventeen year old high school girls born on the same day of the same year, 22-9-1920, two hours apart, but in different countries. Not only they have the same birth date, the same name, they look alike, both play the piano, both are accomplished swimmers. Another case in point is: Two men born on 27-4-1902, one at 12-15 a.m. (Banaras) and the other at 10-38 a.m. (Tanjore). There is approximately 10 hours difference in the actual time of birth. Yet they found that their lives presented the following striking similarities: (*a*) Both have a chronic catarrhal condition of the throat. (*b*) Both have exceptional eyesight. (*c*) The fathers of both are contractors. (*d*) Grandfathers of both had accidents to their feet followed by infection and death. (*e*) The father's mother died when the father was about 5 years old. (*f*) Both had two sisters and one brother. (*g*) Both are interested in the scientific study of astrology.

It may be of interest to readers to know that both Emerson and Lvtton were born on 25-5-1803 at

1–18 p.m. (Boston) and 8 a.m. (London) respectively. Both Emerson and Lytton became men of letters of much distinction. Each had an influence on the politics of his time. Each wrote and published poetry during much of his life. Each drew inspiration from his mother to follow a career of letters. Emerson has Mercury, the intellectual planet in the 10th in his own place while the philosophical Jupiter is in Lagna. Whereas Lytton has the sensual planet Venus in the 10th and the emotional planet Moon in Lagna. Here is the difference. On account of the stress of Jupiter and Mercury respectively on Lagna and the 10th, Emerson's field was philosophy and he wrote for the elect—those who were willing to think deeply. Lytton on the other hand wrote for the common people, choosing for his field drama and fiction consistent with the predominance of lunar and Venus influences on Lagna and the 10th respectively. The following may be noted as indicating more or less parallel events with slight differences in the nature of the results.

Emerson was elected Assistant Preacher in 1829, while Lytton attained his first prominence in 1828 as a novelist through 'Pelham.' In 1831, Lytton had lot of difficulty with his wife from whom he separated, the separation being made legal in 1836. Emerson lost his wife in 1837. The Jupiter–Venus disposition in Emerson's chart gives a clue to his intellectual attainments. He worked for the removal of bigotry, revision of the narrow Christian theological concepts and broadening of views. In 1872 Emerson's health failed and he died in 1882 while Lytton died in 1873. Note the relative strengths of the 8th house in both the horoscopes accounting for the difference in their respective periods of longevity.

We have two more outstanding charts to consider as an illustration of the identity of birth dates. Both Abraham Lincoln and Charles Darwin were born on the same day, *viz.*, 12-2-1809. Charles Darwin's birth-time is not known. Lincoln was born in Kentucky between 7 and 11 a.m. What Lincoln accomplished in the abolition of bodily slavery, Darwin accomplished in the abolition of mental slavery in the Western intellectual world. Each has left a name in his own particular sphere which posterity would gratefully remember. They felt and did that they were friends of all men and they directed their efforts towards acquiring information which the world at large might benefit. Between the lives of Abraham Lincoln and Charles Darwin, there are outstanding parallels, as they were born on the same day of the same year. The departments of life affected by the influences are determined by the positions of planets in houses and Navamsas which depended upon the time of day of birth and therefore there will necessarily be equally outstanding differences in the kind of fortunes attracted to certain departments of their lives. Lincoln lost his mother at the age of 9 as also Darwin. Round the world journey by Darwin began in 1831. Lincoln too took an epochal voyage. The two disliked their studies. Lincoln was assassinated in his 56th year whereas Darwin died in his 73rd year. The times of birth being different, the periods of life in which one had fortune proved unfortunate for the other and *vice versa*. We can cite a number of instances to show that parallelism prevailed in respect of the lives of persons born on the same date, month and year.

VIII

FUTILITY OF FATALISTIC DOCTRINE

Any number of further proofs in support of the validity of astrology can be adduced, but we feel that we have given enough evidence in favour of a rational system of scientific foreknowledge and the subject is deserving of impartial examination and ready acceptance. Astrology can never be considered as a relic of the pseudo-scientific snobbery of the middle ages. The great Kepler, who formulated the mathematical principles of the constitution of the solar system, which were afterwards proved by Newton, said about astrology: "A most unfailing experience of the course of mundane events in harmony with the changes occurring in the heavens has instructed and compelled my unwilling belief." These words of Kepler, says Sepharial, "embody a sober conviction from experience altogether in keeping with the scientific reputations of this great genius," and it is sheer presumption on the part of uninformed critics of astrology to "repudiate this dictum by ascribing the belief to delusion and superstition, or the remarkable prediction of well-known astrologers to *coincidence*". A little reflection will suggest to the average thinking mind that a series of coincidences makes a law. "The ignorant speak of laws if they were compelling forces in the universe. They are in fact nothing but our mental perception of the correlated successiveness of events. Law is a mental concept—not a cosmic energy.

A single bonafide prediction, which was true as to time and nature of event would establish an *a priori* argument for the scientific value of astrology if it could be shown—as it certainly can—that the prediction was made from mathematical calculation of planetary configurations and that the event predicted could not have been foretold otherwise.

Summing up, we find that astrology is not only a most fascinating intellectual study but is a remarkable tool for scrutinising the fringe of future events. As an historical phenomenon it is unique in allowing us to fathom the mentality of more or less distant cultures in space as well as in time. Astrology cannot be called a science in its narrow sense because science deals only with material objects. Yet astrology is based upon scientific data. Any subject that deals with life objects cannot be called a science. Astrology is an applied science and therefore becomes an art. We have also shown that modern scientific thinking is in such great confusion that it can say nothing definitely against determinism or fate. "Chance in nature baffles a complete comprehension and appears meaningless and whimsical as it is not possible to understand natural phenomena." The explanation offered by a dialectical materialist lies in the combination of both chance and necessity. If necessity can be equated with causal relationship, some phenomenon or event can be explained by physical and environmental conditions, but others are again matters of chance. To this extent necessity leads to determinism. Modern science has confessed that, to put in Planck's words, "it is never in a position completely and exhaustively to explain the problems it has to face".

The domain of science is certainly different from the social and political spheres of life. Whatever is latent in our life, that only is revealed by the planetary combinations and that only takes a new form which was lying dormant (Karma) but capable of being enlivened under efficient directing force (Freewill). Thus Karma or Fate or Determinism can exist side by side with freewill. This is the Hindu view and modern concepts are gradually veering towards this important discovery of the ancients.

"Man's action moves on the lines that his own Karma is tracing for him. But his will is free to fashion his Karma. It is determinism to the extent that Karma which is dynamic is shadowed by medieval and unchangeable law of Karma, but life which is guided by freewill does not follow any preordained pattern. Determinism thus appears as a law—a law that operates through changes according to the conditions of each circumstance and environment." Indian philosophy has always denied the existence of a merciless fate which would play with man as it pleases. On the contrary, the Maharshis have unequivocally declared that man has control over his actions but his actions have no control over their results. The horoscope shows a man's character and temperament. If it shows that owing to dominance of Mars and Rahu he would become a criminal, it does not mean he is fated to become so. What it means is that he is just the sort of person who will have criminal tendencies but they can be checked by proper care and training. Suppose an emotional crisis is indicated in a particular year. One can certainly meet the crisis if one knew when it would happen.

Let us be a little more explanatory. One of the first philosophical questions that rises in the mind of a thinker is that of human freedom. If the future of man is determined by the planets and stars, there is nothing that he can achieve by his own effort. His life will be reduced to that of a puppet which has to make every movement in mechanical obedience to the pulls of the operator. Sometimes theologians forget the element of human freedom when glorifying God. They attribute every state of mind, conscious and unconscious, to God's impelling suggestion from within. If this is taken strictly, human freedom disappears. He will not be free to choose between good and evil. In fact the very meaning of good and bad will disappear from the vocabulary of human life. With freedom will disappear all sense of responsibility, moral or other, all sense of sin or wrong-doing, and all aspiration for a nobler state of being.

In this quandary, theologians think of doctrines of the self-limitation of God who lets man have a certain delegated freedom like that of a servant under a master. Absolutist philosophers think of changing the notion of Deity to that of a superpersonal or attributeless (*nirguna*) Being and reduce freedom to the status of *vyavahara* or empirical life, disappearing with the ego itself in the state of *paramartha* or ultimate salvation or moksha or merger. But on the plane of impirical existence, freedom has a real value and is indispensable for the self-regulation of human beings. On this plane, it is not necessarv to assume that astrology destroys the opportunity for human choice.

For astrology reveals only the general influence of the planets and stars on our life careers at different times in our life and development. It reveals tendencies. It reveals good and bad times for certain kinds of choice.

The real situation is that man is partly free and partly determined. His physical nature and his heredity and his position in the cosmos and even in society is determined. He begins with a certain number of facts that he cannot change—his parentage, his nationality, his place in geographical region or country, his temperament, even the life fund of energy—these are his capital.

But he can use this capital in various ways so as to rise higher or sink lower in the scale of value. He can better himself in character and social status or diminish his stature by bad conduct. Man has enough freedom to make or mar himself. He has not enough freedom to command nature and history to suit his fancies.

There is no reason to think that astrology seals the fate of every human being at birth determining every one of his acts of choice every moment of his life. Astrology does not support the idea of kismet or fate or completely determined life for man like a mechanism moved by previously operating causes.

In accordance with the general background of Indian thought, Indian astrology supports the idea of rebirth and karma.

A man's heredity is his inheritance from his own deeds in a previous life. A man's character and potentialities are the summation of his own deeds in previous lives. His present life is influenced by *prarabdha* (operative) karma—tendencies of his previous deeds that have started to function. There are others hidden in his nature ; he can prevent the bad ones among them from taking shape through his choices. He can modify the future while he has to suffer the consequences of the past. Even the past he can convert into strength by the way he faces it by patience and acceptance and determination to change for the future.

Indian astrology envisages the whole cosmos, particularly the Sun and the planets as co-operating with the human individual in moulding his self-formation and self-realisation in the effort to reach Moksha. The universe is a *karya kshetra*—the valley of realisation through deeds. Hence there is room for both freedom and cosmic law in the Indian scheme of things which is shared by Indian astrology.

There is thus a profound view of individuality pervading the Indian vision of life. Each individual has to tread the path of *bhusara samsara* alone from migration to migration or life to life through many societies and many partnerships, using the gift of limited freedom he is endowed with, which is sufficient not to create the universe, but to achieve self-realisation through *jnana* (knowledge), *bhakti* (devotion), *karma* (action) and *lokaseva* (service to humanity).

Thus astrology in India is part of the whole of Indian culture and civilisation and plays an integral part in guiding life for all at all stages of life.

Astrology can be studied with advantage, to helf medicine, agriculture, meteorology and psychology. The only thing is, one should not attempt to make astrology fatalistic and to use it as a means of evading the responsibilities of freewill. In the wide range of physical science there is no question of higher national importance than astrology. [48]"So far from a belief in astrology leading to fatality, it is the neglect of astrology that tends to fatality,

48 *A Text-Book of Astrology* by Dr. A. J. Pearce.

for the laws of nature go on working until the catastrophe arrives which might have been foreseen, and its effects mitigated, had the warning of the heavens been attended to by statesmen and philosophers."

One of the most important uses of astrology is the direction of education and selection of a profession. How often do we not come across misfits? Can any modern science pretend to say that it can show the vocation for which one is best fitted? Education is wasted because millions of people pursue wrong vocations. If modern education cannot enable parents totell their children, what they can do best, then the whole curriculum of study requires to be thoroughly overhauled. An astrologer can discover on the very day when the child is born, whether there would be any aptitude for physics or philosophy.

A few words about astrology and modern psychology and I shall close this chapter. The Hindu undoubtedly deserve the credit for having discovered an astrological-*cum*-psychological classification of human beings which has endured for all these years.

The astrological classification is based upon marked differences of emotional and physical characteristics though the play "of emotion forms the most frequent and obviously striking feature of any behaviour". It is noteworthy therefore that the position of the Moon in the horoscope is supremely important inasmuch as the Moon is the karaka of mind and all the forces released by the play of our emotions. To all external appearance—anatomical and morphological—there is no difference between man and man, though Nature has been perhaps careful to see that no two human faces, except in very rare instances, have the same appearance. Similarly a careful observation extending over long intervals of time has revealed that difference is perceptible between different organs of different individuals. Thus A may have a long nose ; B, snubbed nose and so on so that consistent with these variations, differences in the olfactory powers may be noticed. Astrological writers have distinctly recognised four types based on the predominance of the earthy, fiery, watery or airy elements. Here 'element' does not mean the 'element' of modern science. A knowledge of the psychological make-up of a person based on the astrological qualification is not an insignificant factor inasmuch as it analyses what you are. Of course, the twelve zodiacal types aim at a sharper characterisation of certain typical differences.

The emotional behaviour of man is traced by modern psychologists to what is called the 'affect personality'. 'Affect' is not the only thing that is characteristic of mankind. The Moon's position in the horoscope reveals the 'affect personality' while the sign in which the ascendant falls and the lord of the sign reveal the real personality—"psychological functions veiled in obscurity, and scarcely discernible to the majority of the people." We do not require a modern psychologist to teach us the difference between 'affect' and 'real' personality for these have been already explained, may be in euphemistic language, by ancient astrological writers. When considering the psychological personality of person, due care is taken to see that the physical peculiarities are also impressed.

It is a fact that we are in the habit of justifying "ourselves to any one who holds us responsible for an emotional act by saying that we acted only on impulse" and we would not have done so if we had not been in that emotional condition. In this justification lies an attempt to distinguish oneself from one's own 'affect'. Again if a man judges us by our 'affect' or emotion we say he lacks understanding. In other words, in judging a man, factors other than the emotional ones are also important. Psychologists call the 'real' personality as the ego which is entirely different from the emotional personality. The emotional personality may be a higher one as in instances of generosity, sacrifice, etc., but these cannot be sustained. Now the Moon indicates the 'emotional personality' while the Lagna or the ascendant indicates the true or ego personality. The Moon signifies sensation, instincts, impulses, cautiousness, imagination and changeableness. The true personality is that which is born into this world in a physical body. It brings with it tendencies to types of thought, feeling, and action, in-born and untaught, being derived from its past career as a soul. These innate faculties are expanded and increased by its experiences of this life.

We have attempted to draw the distinction between the two types of personalities with a view to emphasising the need for a correct appreciation of the Lagna factor as different from the Moon factor.

Astrology teaches us that in spite of a great variety of motives and tendencies, certain groups of individuals, characterised by an obvious conformity in their manner of motivation can be differentiated. A knowledge of the astrological type to which one belongs will be highly useful in adjusting his social, sexual and psychological life in such a way that he can follow the line of least resistance.

Though every personality belongs to one of the twelve zodiacal types and is evolving under its influence yet, one can never give a description of a type, "which absolutely applies to one individual despite the fact that thousands might in a certain sense be strikingly characterised by it. Conformity is one side of the man while uniqueness is the other".

In our above observations, we have merely dealt with the psychological aspect of the "real" and "affect" personalities ; but in the astrological aspect, a more comprehensive account of the personality is clearly revealed.

Modern psychologists have recognised three types, *viz.*, (*a*) sensation types, (*b*) thinking types, and (*c*) feeling types. According to Jung, people belonging to 'sensation type' bother themselves very little "about the possibilities which lie hidden in a situation". Those belonging to the 'thinking type' "cannot adapt themselves to a situation which they cannot comprehend intellectually". Those belonging to the third type "give themselves up wholly to the lure of possibilities". Of course this type-classification is very general.

Astrology is not merely the summation of psychology, but it is certainly intimately connected with psychological concepts. In fact, Dr. Jung assures recognition for astrology in the following words :

"Astrology is assured of recognition from psychology, without further restrictions, because astrology represents that summation, of all the psychological knowledge of antiquity." We said above that astrology is the science of sciences for it refers to many things besides psychology—from weather and crop forecasts to State matters and individual affairs. Nor astrology is to be identified in its essence with any experimental or empirical science. Just as mathematics is the organising principle of science dealing with inanimate matter so also astrology is the organising principle of such sciences as deal with life and significance in relation to all living bodies. Bertrand Russel says that "the whole practical utility of knowledge depends upon its power of foretelling the future". Since astrology answers this requirement it must be considered universal knowledge and superior to other branches which apply only to a definite period of time, during which there has been continuous observation.

The use of astrology has been hinted at already. Coming to the functions of astrology, the most important one is that it dispenses with the text-book maxims of ethics and prudence and shows you a way out of deadlocks or blind alleys. Belief in astrology really leads to a new kind of morality. It is certainly different from and more liberating in many respects than the ethical limitations of the ordinary men. Astrology postulates an unending chain of existences, a sort of perpetual seesaw which, amongst a seeming waste of incredible energy, contributes to the conservation of the universal sum-total. It promotes a theoretic appreciation of the Advaita doctrine, for the man who is on top today is found at the bottom tomorrow ; neither of the results is due to sheer volition on his part, but apparently predetermined consequence of the perpetual movement of the wheel. We are not all of us courageous nihilists. We therefore find some petty consolation for our failures in life by attributing them to the stars. Other compensations which astrology offers us are no less valuable. If we are foretold a period of calamity or trouble, advance intimation has the effect of preparing us to break the back of the misfortune by meeting it halfway, and taking it unawares.

The importance of astrology in the social life of man is manifold. Human needs and aspirations furnish a continuous motive power for astrological inquiry. We can divide the needs of a human being in society into several grades of urgency to each of which astrology has a definite relation. The dynamic needs of human society find the motive force in political movements the trend of which can be clearly ascertained by astrological considerations. The pre-knowledge would be a great asset to humanity. Mortality and illness rates can be easily ascertained and steps taken to prevent such happenings and control disease. Man breeds at haphazard, and the resulting changes in quantity and quality of men have the most violent social repercussions. All these developments can be ascertained with the aid of astrology so that the ultimate happiness of men may be ensured. In fact, there are large tasks for mankind to undertake. Astrology helps realisation of all these ideals. The secret value of astrology lies in the fact that you are asked to follow the line of least resistance so that maximum success may be attained with minimum effort.

Some are curious to know "the official reaction of the Marxist or the communist to the subject of astrology". We are inclined to the view that the communists must have nothing but contempt for astrology, since it postulates a future state of existence which is repugnant to the materialist view of the universe. They dream of the apotheosis of the common man by simple, incendiary means : but forget that the moment he becomes uncommon, he becomes the arch-enemy of the Communist State. The pure Communist, if one can get at one, must be of heroic mould. For he labours with all the accumulated zeal and arrested momentum of centuries, to establish his millennium for the span of a generation. He mav no doubt entertain the belief that the missionary fervour that has prompted him to action will continue to prompt others after him, and that his proletarian El Dorado will endure for ever, once he sets it on its feet. This is in reality the old fallacy in a new garb ; the old mysticism which believed in a survival of personality transferred to an equally untenable faith in the survival of a State or society. How little justification there is for such a pleasing fiction will be evident from the persistent sea-change which Communism has been undergoing in the home of its birth, from the date of its birth.

IX

*CAN ASTROLOGY PREDICT EARTHQUAKES ?

On 28th July 1976 China suffered one of the worst catastrophes in its history. An exceptionally violent earthquake hit a very densely populated industrial region, 150 kilometers east of Peking. The city of Tangshan was reported in total ruin. At least 1,00,000 people are said to have lost their lives. The quake damaged buildings in Peking, and fearing more shocks might follow, Peking's six million people stayed out of their houses. The tremors were said to be of such magnitude that not only damage was caused to Peking's Hall of the Peoples but several dams, bridges and peasants' houses were destroyed in many parts of north-east China.

Apart from the huge loss of life and property and the need for diversion of resources to rehabili-

---

* Editorial by the Author reprinted from October 1976 issue of THE ASTROLOGICAL MAGAZINE.

tate the areas damaged, it seems, the earthquake in China had political implications also. The impact of the earthquake on "superstitious peasants" worried the Government, because of the anticipation (of the peasants) that this natural phenomenon "presaged a national calamity or a change of dynasty as had been interpreted when monarchs ruled the land".

Scientists, as usual, are not agreed, as to the exact cause of earthquakes. Though the Russians claimed about 15 years ago to have made an important discovery in the field of earthquake prediction, nothing further has been known as to whether any reliable system of forecasting earthquakes was developed. Their discovery that the "ratio between the velocities of natural wave motions through the ground dropped significantly days before an earthquake and then returned to normal just before it took place" is said to be an important step towards the direction of making earthquake forecasts. But no two scientists seem to agree either regarding the cause of earthquakes or methods of forecast.

After the Koyna disaster in 1967, the "water-load" theory was advanced by the French scientist Rothe and later by the Indian scientists Gupta and Rastogi. Then a team of Unesco experts found that "the impounded water was not the cause". Subsequently Dr. Mc Kenzic of Cambridge and

Dr. Brunne of California Universities advanced the theory that "earthquakes lubricate themselves at an early stage and then spread rapidly". John Michell of Cambridge University attributed the vibratory movements in earthquakes to what he called "elastic waves traversing the crust". While seismology is said to be a "science" and the seismograph is capable of registering even distant earthquakes, of course after they have happened, we have yet to hear of a seismologist ever having predicted correctly the occurrence of an earthquake.

The astonishing fact is that most of the scientists, engaged in earthquake studies, do not seem to take an integrated view of what is happening on or above the earth's crust.

Of all the known sciences, Astrology alone takes into cognisance that all phenomena including the occurrence of earthquakes are regulated by planetary movements. Such a theory is not an idle fancy especially in the light of the findings of at least some of the scientists that earthquakes can be triggered by solar activity. For instance Dr. Anderson a seismologist of the California Institute of Technology does not look at seismic events in isolation. In an analysis of the 17-year period of violence (1897 to 1914) "during which there were quakes of a magnitude greater than eight on the Richter scale" he saw that "tsunamis (tidal waves 30 metres high) increased in number, the length of the day changed, that is, the earth's rotation slowed down, the world's mean temperature rose by one degree and the 'Chandler-wobble' was at its peak". He says further that these were interlinked. All these geo-physical events are part of a large energy-chain. The periodicity of the Chandler-wobble is 40 years and this is said to explain the 1950 and 1952 earthquakes in Assam and Kamchatka.

Therefore the vagaries of the Sun are not without consequences for our planet, let alone for the human species on it. Danjon, Director of the observatory at Paris, announced that during January, February and March 1963, the days had been shorter. And it is wroth while noting that Danjon announced an important deviation in the earth's rotation before the disaster of Agadir.

If as scientists claim to have discovered, the Sun's vagaries alter the duration of the day, it is reasonable to assume that they may even induce earthquakes. In 1968 astronomer Trellis showed evidence that the "gravitational effect of the planets moderates the eleven-year solar-activity cycle." Consequently it is the Sun and the planetary juxtapositions that could afford a mathematically workable method to forecast all natural phenomena, including of course earthquakes.

The ancient classic *Garga Samhita* traces the quaking of the earth to "Ketus" or dark spots on the Sun. And this theory is gaining confirmation amongst a section of western scientists not intent on sticking to orthodox theories.

Chile was rocked by a deadly earthquake in May 1960. And two days earlier the scientists had found that a huge spot was passing over the central meridian of the Sun and they thought that the spot had caused the disaster.

Many scientists have started attributing—though they may not publicly admit this—the periodicity of solar spots to planetary configurations. Indeed it is not the Sun alone who provokes the earthquake shocks. The other planets and the Moon also stimulate the activity of the subterranean forces. These scientists have also found that a comparison of the graphs of solar activity, the occurrence of earthquakes and the velocity of earth's rotation reveal that curves are distinctly similar thus showing a definite connection. Dr. Stetson comes forward with the theory that "when the orbit of the Moon is in a particularly close relation to the epicentres of earthquake sources, the strain on the earth at that point is at its maximum and therefore the crust of the earth is likely to break producing an earthquake". In other words we can say that Dr. Stetson has found that the Moon's movements have something to do with the occurrence of earthquakes. Other planets, especially the Sun, Mars, Saturn and Jupiter are really responsible for earthquakes while the Moon gives the finishing touch.

Dr. Rudolph Tomaschek, a geophysicist from the University of Munich. "after checking the places of all the planets during 134 severe earthquakes" has reported what he calls, "a relationship between the positions of planets especially Uranus and earthquakes". It is an astrological dictum that more earthquakes occur when two or more planets are in line to the earth and especially about the times of Full Moon and New Moon.

As early as the beginning of Kaliyuga (3100 B.C.) Parasara has observed thus : *Arka chandra grahaana graha vikrithacharajamscha kampana hayulu* : meanning that when the course of a planet is disturbed from the normal path owing to the attractive force of other planets there is a shaking of the planet which is perceived as an earthquake. Though Gargi says that earthquakes are due to volcanic eruptions Parasara's view seems to be more reasonable as it can be proved astrologically. In fact, planetary action as an exciting cause of earthquakes is only doubted by those who have never made any fair and complete inquiry into it. Aristotle placed on record the fact that it sometimes happens that there is an earthquake about the time of eclipse of the Moon.

By means of monthly lunations and solar and lunar eclipses, one could predict earthquakes. When a number of superior planets are in conjunction or in the same declination or in the same latitude, there will be earthquakes. Several planets in the Tropics also give rise to this phenomenon. Eclipses falling at quadrants to Jupiter, Saturn or Mars also produce earthquakes. The area of the occurrence is generally indicated by the zodiacal sign in which the above combinations occur or by the sign which has the conjunction or the eclipse on the meridian or the Nadir. The locality is also indicated in places where Saturn or Jupiter is in the meridian.

A study of the available astrological literature reveals that (*a*) earthquakes generally occur at or near the times of eclipses and new and full-Moon days ; (*b*) the time of occurrence is generally between midnight and sunrise or midday and sunset ; (*c*) planets, especially the major ones, occupy either mutual quadrants, trines or are in mutual conjunction or opposition ; (*d*) the ascendant, the 4th, the 7th, the 8th, the 12th or the 10th house at the place of the occurrence will be generally afflicted ; (*e*) the asterism of the day may belong to *prithvi* (earth) or *vayu* (air) category; and (*f*) the Moon and Mercury will be in close conjunction or in the same constellation.

These are general combinations and stand to be tested in the light of the earthquake occurrences in the past.

The Tokyo earthquake which occurred on 1-9-1923 resulted in the death of 1,40,000 people and destruction of most of Tokyo and Yokohama. There

	Moon		
Ketu	Chart No. 1		
	RASI		Mars Rahu Sun Venus
	Ascdt.	Jupiter	Sat. Merc.

	Jupiter Ketu	Mercury	Mars
	NAVAMSA		Sun Venus Saturn
		Rahu	Moon Ascdt.

was a lunar eclipse on 26th August involving Leo-Aquarius, the point rising at Tokyo being aspected by Mars. The quake struck Tokyo as the Moon entered the constellation of Bharani ruled by Yama, the lord of death. On the day of the earthquake, the 10th degree of Scorpio was rising at Tokyo, the constellation involved being that of Saturn, the ascendant being aspected by two malefics and Mars being exactly in the 10th house. It will be seen that there is a conglomeration of four planets in the 10th house. But seven planets are clustered within an arc of seventy-two degrees. When such a clustering takes place, earthquakes and cyclones happen. But to identify the time and locality is still a difficult matter even for astrological savants.

		Ascdt.	
Venus	Chart No. 2		Ketu
Sun, Moon Mars, Rahu Mercury Saturn	RASI		
		Jupiter	

Ketu			
	NAVAMSA		Mars
Sun Moon Merc.			Saturn
		Jupiter Venus	Rahu Ascdt.

On 15-1-1934, a massive quake occurred in Bihar. It was a new-Moon day and seven planets were in configuration in the sign of Capricorn. The Sun, Mars, Venus and the Moon were all in exact conjunction in the constellation of Uttarashadha ruled by the Sun lord of the 8th. It will be noted that the earthquake actually occurred after the Moon entered Capricorn. The occurrnce of this earthquake had been forecast by a number of Indian astrologers, long before the event happened. The sign involved is earthy. Shocks were also felt in Mexico and Chile ruled by Capricorn. For China the deadly conjunction falls in the Nadir. The conjunction and the eclipse have both taken place in Capricorn. Mercury is in close conjunction with the Moon.

The Agadir earthquake which occurred just before midnight on 29-2-1960 left nearly 12,000 people dead.

The quake on the 29th February followed the new Moon on the 26th in Aquarius, an airy sign. On the 28th the Moon joined Mercury and on the 29th the Moon was exactly in a kendra from Saturn. The

Moon Mercury Ketu			
Sun	Chart No. 3 RASI		
Mars Venus			
Saturn Jupiter		Ascdt.	Rahu

Sun		Ascdt. Mars	Jupiter Venus
	NAVAMSA		
			Mercury Ketu
	Saturn Moon		

disposition of Rahu, Saturn, Jupiter, the Moon and Mercury in mutual kendras is significant.

Several thousand square miles of north-west Iran were devastated by a severe earthquake on [a]2-9-1962, the first shock having occurred at 10-55 p.m. 75 towns and villages were ruined and ten thousand people were killed. The Lagna at the time of the quake was Taurus an earthy sign and the earthquake followed in the wake of the new Moon on 29th August. The most significant factor is the Moon passed over Mercury on 1st September. Jupiter is in the 10th and Mars and Jupiter in mutual trines. Mercury and Mars are again in mutual trines.

Coming to the recent Chinese earthquake, the U.S. Geological Survey, Colorado, estimated the magnitude of the first quake (which occurred on [b]28-7-1976) at 1-15 a.m. (I.S.T.) or 3-45 a.m. Peking Time as 8.2 points "on the open-ended Reichter scale" and said that it was the world's strongest for 12 years.

---

a. *Rasi* : Taurus—Ascendant ; Gemini—Mars ; Cancer—Rahu ; Leo—the Sun ; Virgo—the Moon and Mercury ; Libra—Venus ; Capricorn—Ketu and Saturn ; and Aquarius—Jupiter.

Navamsa : Taurus—Mercury, Saturn and Ketu ; Cancer—Ascendant ; Virgo—the Sun and the Moon ; Scorpio—Venus and Rahu ; and Aquarius —Jupiter and Mars.

b. The Sun 102° 49′ ; the Moon 112° 28′ ; Mars 140° 41′ ; Mercury 115° 47′ ; Jupiter 34° 46′ ; Venus 113° 44′ ; Saturn 104° 6′ : Rahu 196° 8′ ; and Ascendant 85° 2′.

	Ketu	Jupiter	Asc. 25-2
	Chart No. 4 RASI		Sat. Moon Sun Mer. Venus
			Mars
		Rahu	

		Ascdt.	
Merc. Venus Ketu Jupit.	NAVAMSA		
			Ketu
	Saturn	Sun Mars	

It is said that Chinese scientists had predicted a few weeks earlier of the impending earthquake. According to Dr. C. Barry Raeigh, geo-physicist and his colleagues in the team that visited China a month earlier, the radio stations in Peking had been warning the people about the natural calamity. It is also acknowledged the Government could not give any advance warning to the people to stay out of doors.

One implication of the disaster is, the earthquake-predicting system might have failed to work. But the American visitors, referred to above, learnt that the Chinese are able to forewarn on the basis of "earthquake lights" or "ground glows" discerned in their laboratories and also by peculiar animal behaviour. Geophysicists say the Chinese theory of "ground glows" is convincing "because of the considerable release of electricity'' during the earthquakes, which means a correlation between positions of planets and the electrical disturbances. The American visitors did not wish to dismiss the theory of unusual animal behaviour also. Two hours before the quake tigers at the Tienstin zoo began acting strangely. There was panic among the chickens. Pigs refused to enter their holes and horses and sheep ran about in a frenzy. How wonderful is nature's earthquake sensors !

In Chart No. 4, the Lagna is Gemini an airy sign. There is a five-planet combination in the second house affecting the 8th or house of destruction. Jupiter and Mars are in mutual square. The earthquake on the 28th followed on the wake of the new Moon on the 26th. The most important feature is again the closeness of the Moon and Mercury. On the new Moon day, the Moon was in Punarvasu and the earthquake occurred when he entered Aslesha, the constellation held by Mercury. It seems evident that the Moon and Mercury have a significant role to play in causing earthquakes.

On the day of the Chinese earthquake except Jupiter (and the shadowy planets Rahu and Ketu) the rest are clustered within an arc of 38°.

In the January 1978 issue of THE ASTROLOGICAL MAGAZINE, we had observed based on the total lunar eclipse on 16-9-1978 "that there is the probability of a major earthquake about the area of Iran". On the very same night of the eclipse day a powerful earthquake hit Iran killing 10,000 people.

From the charts given above certain basic astrological facts bearing on the occurrence of earthquakes thrust themselves prominently before us. If according to modern science everything in life is electrical in nature, then the tiniest atom and the great cosmos, including the planets, the earth and the Sun, are charged bodies with a field about them and therefore subject to certain mathematical laws. We do not know whether earthquakes are caused by gravitational effects of the Sun, the Moon and other planets. The grouping of planets in certain signs show significant correspondence with earthquakes. Planets may affect the force-field of the earth and cause earthquakes. In fields of knowledge such as predicting earthquakes astrology has much to offer to contemporary seismology. If only modern scientists could keep their minds open, the accumulated wisdom of astrology could be of great assistance.

The loss of life and damage to property are the chief features of a great earthquake. The number of persons killed in a few minutes is indeed appalling. Fatalists may want to know what would be the use of knowing when earthquake and other natural calamities occur.

The answer is, it is certainly not possible to prevent the occurrence of earthquakes. But we may endeavour to lessen the destructive power of earthquakes by forecasting their occurrence in advance.

Though by no means conclusive, astrological data lend support to the theory of correlation of planetary configurations with natural calamities.

X

ASTROLOGY AND WEATHER FORECASTING

For Bangalore, midnight Tuesday 22nd October 1975 was a nightmare because "a downpour the like of which it has not seen perhaps for decades descended on it all on a sudden leaving behind an unprecedented trail of suffering, tribulation and misery". Within a brief span of an hour and a half it had rained almost four inches rendering nearly 5000 homeless, in just one locality. Wholesale grain dealers said "as much as Rs. 15 lakhs worth of stocks had been washed away in the mini floods. Hundreds of bales of expensive textiles and thousands of bags of cement got under water."

The morning's newspapers carried the Forecast: "generally cloudy with sunny intervals. **One or two showers likely in the evening or night"** (bold ours). There was no indication of even ordinary rain let alone the deluge. The same phenomenon happened recently at Bombay. The meteorological forecast was "some showers" but the city had a deluge. Yet meteorology continues to be a respectable "science". The present-day meteorologists seem to think that to forecast weather is their exclusive privilege. Meteorology, so far as prediction of weather is concerned, has retrograded rather than improved. Let the modern meteorologists study their records of observations with the conjunctions and aspects of planets and their movements in different constellations. Such a study would rescue meteorology from its present hopeless and helpless state.

It is possible for astrology to forecast weather more accurately than meteorology? This is the question most frequently asked by the laymen. Because of their training and *a priori* considerations, some scientists have a tendency to disregard a fact of great importance, *viz.*, astrologically it is possible to forecast weather, much more accurately than meteorology. In astrology as in other fields of scientific study, the great temptation that exists is the urge to deal with the problem by over-simplifying it. Thus for instance, the western astrologer might stick to the proposition that a certain aspect between two major planets might cause storms. This inference is indeed an over-simplification and not consistent with the techniques employed in Hindu astrology. The comprehensive methods of weather forecasting are to be found in ancient classics and they should be understood and applied through systematic investigation and research, as otherwise our performances may fall in line with the reckless performances of the meteorologists.

According to the theory of astrology propounded by ancient sages, all phenomena including rainfall, floods, etc., are regulated by planetary movements. Of late some of the scientists have been indirectly endorsing astrological theories. For instance in 1962 Glen W. Brier of the Massachusetts Institute of Technology announced the discovery of a remarkable correlation between the phases of the Moon and rainfall in U.S.A. Similar results were arrived at independently by E. E. Adderley of the Radio-physics Division of the CSIRO in Australia. When precipitation data were plotted in terms of the Moon's phases, it was found that heavy rain occurred most frequently about four days after full Moon and reached a secondary peak about 4 days after new Moon. In other words the greatest amount of rain fell when the Moon was either 45° or 225° from the Sun. These findings were based on the study of data taken from U.S. Weather Bureau precipitation statistics covering the period 1900-1949 and dates of maximum rainfall for each calendar month.

It should be within the keen observation of a

student of astrology that rain tends to increase when the Moon is at one of its nodes irrespective of its phase. Whether the mechanism involved is gravitational or electrical we do not know. But there is no doubt that a clear correlation persists between the movements of the Moon and variations in quantities of rainfall.

A perusal of the Sanskrit astrological works such as *Brihat Samhita* should convince any doubting Thomas that weather forecasts amongst ancient Indian rulers played an important part in public administration. Meteorology was a distinctly comprehensive science and Varahamihira deserves much credit for his writings embodying the important results of observation and experiment carried on through many centuries.

To the ancient Hindu astronomers, the weather indications of one single day in a year form the subject of so much calculation in determining the future agricultural prospect of the land, while to the inexperienced eye of a western man of science, the day appears as indifferent as any other day of the year. This suggests that modern science is still far behind in her investigation of the laws of nature.

The science of weather forecasting developed by the sages explains the cause as well as the effect of atmospheric changes through repeated occurrences of planetary positions.

Exhaustive rules for forecasting weather have been given in ancient books, but we shall give here only a few of them. Those who wish to make a detailed study of astro-meteorology can refer to works like *Garga Samhita*, *Brihat Samhita*, etc.

The positions of planets in the north of the celestial equator are said to have a definite influence on the movements of the pressure-systems for periods of whole seasons. It must always be understood that there is a "human element" that gives the wrong results and that it is not the fault of nature. It is common-sense that we cannot forecast a flood, even when the planetary combinations favour it, in the middle of a desert. Nor can we forecast a cold wave in the tropics because such things do not generally happen. While making forecasts one should clearly take note of climatology and geography of the land.

It has been found that when Jupiter is in perihelion there is great drought and when in aphelion more dampness and cold weather than usual. When a planet enters Cancer it will influence more the weather in the northern hemisphere while the southern hemisphere is more influenced when the sign is Capricorn. The season, time of the month, day, etc., should all be considered before a forecast is made. Generally when the Sun conjoins Mercury, the weather is given to windy spells along coastal areas and increase the depth of high and low pressure systems. With Venus, the weather gives rise to increase in rain or snow. With Mars, the weather becomes warmer and especially in Aries, the summer becomes very severe. With Jupiter the weather becomes dry and sometimes as the season changes it will bring drought. With Saturn the pressure is stagnate over long periods and colder than normal for the season. With Rahu or Ketu, the weather is severe for the season and changeable.

When the Sun and the Moon are in neutral asterisms there will be winds ; when they are in feminine asterisms there will be lightning and phosphorescence ; and when the Sun occupies a feminine asterism, and the Moon a masculine asterism, or *vice-versa* there will be rains.

At the time of the Sun's Ingress into Gemini, if Venus occupies the 2nd or 12th from the rising sign and when at the same time, the Moon occupies a watery Navamsa in any sign, there will be copious rains during the year in question (Aries to Pisces is a year). When the Sun, the Moon, Mars, Saturn and Rahu cross the watery signs in transit and

Mercury and Venus conjoin a Sthula Rasi, there will be very heavy rains.

When the Sun, Mercury and Venus occupy the same sign and the same Navamsa, there will be heavy rains. But if these planets occupy the same Rasi (sign) and Navamsa and they happen to be watery signs, the rains will be all the more heavy.

When the Sun occupies an earthy sign and the Moon, Mercury and Venus occupy watery signs, and at that time if a rainbow is seen in the western side, then also there will be plentiful rains.

In 'Varsha Ritu' (July–August) a rainbow in the eastern side does not give rain. In the other 'ritus' (seasons) a rainbow in the east will bring in 'rains'. A rainbow in the west during the Varsha Ritu brings in a pour.

When the mock Sun is visible to the north of the Sun's disc, there will be rain ; to the south there will be a tempest ; and on both sides, a 'flood' will come in. To the top of the Sun's disc means some danger to the king, and below it will mean some calamittes to the people.

When it rains on the new Moon days and the days succeeding them (Prathipada days) there will be good rainfall during that bright half of the lunar month. If it rains on full Moon days and the dark Prathipada (1st lunar date) there will be no rains in the dark half. In both Pakshas (half lunar months) when it rains during the first 15 ghatikas (6 hours) in Dwiteeya (2nd lunar day) and the last 15 ghatikas in Prathipada (1st lunar day) there will be copious rains during those Pakshas (fortnights). When it rains only a little on those days, rains will be scarce during those Pakshas (fortnights). If it does not rain then, there will be no rain during that Paksha (fortnight).

When the winds blow from the north-east in the evening (sandhya) of the full Moon day of Ashadha (July-August) month, there will be downpour and consequent luxuriant vegetable life during the ensuing year.

When it rains on the 4th lunar day of the dark half of Ashadha (July-August) and on the day ruled by Poorvabhadra in the same month, there will be luxuriant vegetation during the year ahead.

When the 5th lunar day of the bright half of the luuar month falls on a Sunday (in Ashadha) there will be a little rain. If it is on a Monday, there will be a downpour. If it is a Tuesday rains will be fierce; Wednesday would bring in a storm; Thursday—general prosperity; Friday—rain and loss; Saturday—there will be misery everywhere.

If the constellation of Rohini coincides with the

10th lunar day (in the month of Ashadha) there will be terrible rains.

The Sun occupies $2\frac{1}{4}$ Nakshatras every month beginning from Aswini (alpha Arietis) making up 12 months from Aries. He occupies Poorvashadha in the month of Sagittarius and stays there for 13 days and 8 hours (13 degrees and 20 minutes). If during the 1st day, all the sky including the Sun is found to be completely covered by dark clouds, there will be rain during the month of Gemini when the Sun occupies Aridra. Similarly, if during the 2nd day all the heavens are found to be dark by clouds, there will be rain during the latter part of Gemini and the first part of Cancer when the Sun will occupy the asterism of Punarvasu. Similarly on the 3rd day, 4th day, 5th day, 6th day and so on till the 14th day, if the same conditions prevail, there will be rains during the succeeding months when the Sun will be in Pushyami, Aslesha, Makha, Pubba, till Moola in regular succession.

The above information is useful giving long-range forecasts which appear to have been a speciality with our ancient meteorologists. If the heavens are clear, then there will be no rain.

Rains can be expected in the following periods:-

(*a*) When the combustion periods of the various planets begin and end. (*b*) When the Moon conjoins with other planets. (*c*) Full Moon and New Moon days. (*d*) When the Sun transits Cancer and Capricorn. (*e*) When the Sun occupies the Aridra asterism. When Mercury conjoins Jupiter or Venus or when Jupiter joins Venus there will be rain. When Mars and Saturn join together without any aspect or association of good planets, then danger from fire, lightning and storms can be expected.

We are also enabled to determine the very day of the occurrence of rain from a knowledge of the nature of the clouds during the day. When clouds surrounded by a radiance resembling that of the Moon, white as nectar, with a blue-black spot in the centre, and pouring layers of water pass from west to east or east to west, we can predict that there will be a very heavy shower before long.

If in the rainy season, the sunrise is observed to have a 'halo' in the east and the noon (midday) is marked by the intense heat of the Sun's rays, we can make sure that there will be rain that day. Apart from atmospheric factors, the ancient meteorologists took note of the behaviour of certain animals as indicating immediate rainfall. They are : Cows hasten home to meet their calves. Cats scratch the ground with their claws. Hills shine at a distance and seem to have a blue colouring. The disc of the Moon has a circular red line, the colour being that of the eyes of the hen. Chamelions climb up trees and stare stupidly at the sky. Cows too seem to stare upwards. Cocks crow in the day looking up. Flashes of lightning are marked in the north-east. The Moon is observed to have the colour of honey or of the eyes of parrots or doves. The disc of the Moon, though enveloped in clouds, seems to emanate a radiance round in shape—Prathi Chandra (mock Moon).

We are asked to predict that there will be rains immediately if the following are observed :—

Pearls of thunder crash in the night-time, deep red flashes of lightning are observed during day-time; cold winds blow from the east; young sprouting leaves raise their heads high; birds freely bathe in water or in dust; serpents bask in the sunshine lying on grass; clouds assume the colour of a peacock, parrot, wild crow or chathaka bird and seem to have the shape of waves, hills, tortoise, pigs and fishes.

Evidently, the ancient meteorologists were keen students of nature as they have taken into consideration every kind of phenomenon which indicates a change in the weather.

If the Lagna rising at the time of Aries ingress happens to be a watery sign and is aspected by watery planets there will be proper rains. If the

Rasi is a fiery one and is associated with or aspected by fiery planets, there will be no rain.

When Aries ingress happens to fall on Rohini, Anuradha, Jyeshta, Uttarashadha, Abhijit, Sravana, Dhanishta, the year is known as 'Indra Mandala'. The year will be happy and prosperous. When the Sankramana (solar ingress) falls on Bharani, Krittika, Pushyami, Makha, Pubba, Visakha and Poorvabhadra, the year is known as 'Agni Mandala'. The effect will be fear from fire, poverty everywhere, crops fail and autumn crops are destroyed. When the ingress happens to be on Aswini, Mrigasira, Punarvasu, Uttara, Hasta, Chitta or Swati, then the year has 'Vayu Mandala'. Fear from kings, storms and scarcity of rains will be the result. When the ingress happens to be on Aridra, Aslesha, Moola, Poorvashadha, Satabhisha, Uttarabhadra or Revati then the year has 'Varuna Mandala'. Good rains and general prosperity will ensue.

If the fifth day of the bright half of the lunar month Chaitra falls on Monday or Thursday, rainfall will be equally spread throughout that year ; if on Wednesday, disturbed rains accompanied by winds ; Friday, crops will be destroyed ; Saturday or Tuesday, there will be poor rains.

If the 8th day of the bright half of the lunar month Vaisakha falls on Saturday or Tuesday famine will set in and the year will be marked by absence of regular rains. The constellation Mrigasira or Aridra, rising on the 1st day of the lunar month Jyeshta, produces excellent rains.

The four days commencing from the eighth day in the bright half of the month of Jyeshta (May and June) are known as Vayudharana days—that is days from the winds that blow on which the nature of the health of the pregnancy of the rain clouds might be determined. If in the said bright half of Jyeshta there should be a fall of rain in the four days when the Moon passed through the asterisms from Swati to Jyeshta, there will be rain in the rainy season, *i.e.*, from Sravana to Kartika (August to November). If on the Dharana (rain supporting) days the Sun and the Moon should be covered by wet clouds there will be good rain.

The month of Jyeshta (May–June) seems to be very important for measuring the rainfall. If there should be rain when the Moon passes through certain asterisms from Poorvashadha to Moola in the lunar month of Jyeshta, there will also be rain when the Moon passes through the same asterisms in the rainy season. If there should be no rain in the month of Jyeshta, there will be no rain the rainy season. If there should be a fall of rain when the Moon passes Mrigasira, Chitta, Revati and Dhanishta in

Jyeshta there will be good rain in the rainy season. If there should be a fall when the Moon passes through Satabhisha, Jyeshta and Swati, the subsequent rainfall will be ordinary.

When the Moon passes through the asterism of Rohini in the dark half of the lunar month Ashadha, Rohini Yoga is caused. The astronomer "shall ascertain the direction of the wind at the time when the Moon enters Rohini. He shall divide this day into 9 equal parts (3 hours each) commencing from sunrise—the parts representing severally the eight fortnights of the four months of the rainy season from Sravana to Kartika ; and he shall determine on which month or fortnight and how long there will be rain judging from the direction and duration of the wind. "If on the Rohini Yoga day, the sky should be clear and without clouds and the Sun exceedingly hot, there will be rain in the rainy season". Mankind will not be happy and there will be no rains whatsoever if there should occur unusual phenomena such as meteoric falls, thunderbolts, mockfires, etc., on the Rohini Yoga day.

A careful study of these rules suggests that the transit of the Moon in the constellations of Poorvabhadra and Swati in the lunar month of Jyeshta is highly significant. Observation of the sky, direction of the wind, appearance of mock-light, haloes, comets, lightning, thunderbolts, etc., have all received very careful attention of the ancient writers.

Here is an experiment suggested in an ancient work to note the direction of wind and its predictive use. Of course in its place we can employ the latest modern methods for observing the direction of the wind.

(*a*) "One who wishes to know the direction of the wind should get a thick cloth of 24 feet length and 6 feet width. He should hoist this cloth on a pole measuring 144 feet high firmly fixed to the ground, on the morning of the 15th day of the lunar month Ashadha and observe the 'flag' carefully.

"If the flag flies towards the east (which means the wind blows from the west) crops thrive well during the year ; towards agneya (north-east)—rainfall will be below normal ; south or niruti (south-west)—clouds form but there will be little or no rain ; west—excessive rainfall and strong winds ; vayavya (north-west)—excessive rains and strong winds ; north—enough rains to give good crops ; eesanya (south-east)—destruction of crops by heavy untimely rains." (*b*) When the 7th day of the bright half of the lunar month Ashadha coincides with the 4th quarter of Poorvabhadra, Uttarabhadra or Revati, a clear halo will form around the Sun and the rains will be mixed with heavy winds during the year in question.

According to Hindu meteorology, Venus is closely associated with rainfall. Here are some hints.

(*a*) Rainfall will be below normal in the year in which, during the lunar months of Sravana, Kartika, Margasira, Makha or Jyeshta, Venus sets and a solar eclipse caused by Rahu occurs.

(*b*) There will be unprecedented rainfall resulting in heavy floods when Venus rises heliacally or sets in the constellations of Swati, Visakha and Anuradha.

(*c*) For want of rains, famine will break out when Venus rises or sets in one of the constellations from Jyeshta to Sravana.

(*d*) There will be drought conditions when Venus sets in or retrogrades in Makha or Uttarashadha.

(*e*) When Mars and Saturn are in conjunction, rainfall will be very low.

(*f*) Clouds become scattered and rainfall disturbed, when the Sun, Mars and Venus transit the same sign.

(*g*) If Jupiter joins the above combination, clouds will deliver rains in plenty.

(*h*) When Jupiter retrogrades in Rohini, the year will have less rainfall.

Much rain results when Jupiter is in Pisces while

Venus is in Cancer. Heavy winds occur when they are in any airy triplicity and extreme heat is felt when in a fiery triangle. In an earthy triplicity the climate is rendered very dry, except when Jupiter is strongly aspected by a moist planet at the time of its ingress into an earthy triplicity.

When Mars is in Aries in trine to the Sun in Leo a hot season is made hotter still and warmth added to a cold period. Rain in abundance is shown when they are in a watery triplicity and in conjunction with Venus. Very heavy rainfall follows an eclipse or a great conjunction in Cancer, Scorpio and Pisces and more so if Saturn and Jupiter see each other or they aspect the phenomena referred to.

It is wellknown that when the Sun is in conjunction with Sirius the heat becomes offensive and no rain could be expected unless the Sun is aspected either by Saturn and Jupiter or Venus. When Venus is transiting the area known as Pleiades in Taurus there is much rain and the air is kept cool.

During the cold season Venus in conjunction with Saturn gives rain. In northern and southern latitudes, farther than the Tropics, there will be heavy snow-falls. During the hot season in the equatorial regions there will be rain and hail-storms.

Mercury in conjunction or opposition with Venus gives both sunshine and showers. Real gloomy weather with heavy mists results when Mercury, Mars and Saturn form a trigraha-yoga having the aspect of Venus. Cold, dull weather can be foreseen at a time when Saturn is aspected by either Sun or Mars together with an aspect of Venus.

Jupiter in a watery sign in conjunction with or in opposition to Venus gives short showers and a very cool atmosphere. The people get a new zest for life. Jupiter so placed with an aspect of Saturn in an airy sign produces a windy and wet day. Plenty of rain follows when Mars in Cancer is aspecting Venus in Libra and the rains will continue for several days if the Moon and Jupiter cast their aspect also.

Mars rules thunder and when he is in a fiery sign, there will be terrific thunder without rain. Sometimes lightning also occurs. If he is aspected either by Venus or Saturn heavy rain with large drops of water will pour down accompanied by violent thunder. Whenever the Sun is in conjunction with or in opposition to Saturn the weather is cool (or cold according to the latitude) if Mars or Mercury does not aspects the Sun. Similar indications are noted when Jupiter is in conjunction with or in opposition to Saturn. The aspect of Mars and Saturn produce clear, cool weather with slight showers but Saturn and Venus produce a dull wet time. Any planet separating from an aspect of Jupiter and applying to an aspect of Saturn, reduce the temperature of the air. In latitudes where winter is normal there will be bitter cold winds. Along the equator the temperature will be reduced.

A mild winter can be easily foreseen when at the time of Sun's ingress to Capricorn (along December 22) the Moon or Venus passes over Saturn and joins Jupiter. A very cold, hard, frosty and snowy winter follows if the movement is from Jupiter to Saturn. Astrologers in England and Germany can verify this. Droughts are noticed when Saturn is unaspected in Aries, Leo or Sagittarius.

Strong south-west winds are indicated when Mars or Saturn occupy Gemini, Libra or Aquarius and are in opposition or square to each other. Mars in Gemini and Saturn in Pisces assuredly bring heavy blowing. South-west winds do result when Jupiter is in Aquarius in opposition to Saturn in Leo. North-west monsoon winds are ruled by Saturn and South-west, by Jupiter. When they are in airy signs the direction of the wind is easily ascertained. South-west winds also arise when an eclipse occurs in an airy sign. North winds, Jupiter; easterly, Saturn; western, Mars; southern, Venus; and mixed, Mercury. The air is essentially ruled by the planet which is applying to the Moon after its conjunction, opposition or square with the Sun.

The above methods may look somewhat fantastic to us, educated as we are, according to Western methods, but having due regard for the wisdom of the sages, it would be well to test the truth of their statements. An appeal to facts, if conducted fairly and extended day by day over a sufficient length of time—for a casual observation now and again is not sufficient—is sure to convince the observer that certain planetary positions do actually accompany definite changes in weather and that this occurs too frequently to be dismissed as chance-coincidence.

Modern astronomers and meteorologists would find it more useful and more instructive to watch for and study such coincidences than to confine their observations of Mars and Saturn to the delightful amusement of "testing photometrically and also photographically the lustre of the conjoined planets".

XI

*ASTROLOGY AS AN AID TO MEDICAL SCIENCE

If we closely examine the innumerable combinations listed in ancient classical texts on what is called medical astrology, there would be found to exist an amazing series of parallels between the regular motions of the planets in the solar system of which our earth is a part, and the ebb and flow of physical, mental and emotional phenomena peculiar to human life on earth. Of what use after all, to extend the boundaries of our physical domain, by the discovery of new stars and galaxies if some attempt is not made at the same time to discover the significance of these phenomena, as applied to living beings and their problems of existence and evolution? Today while no serious or systematic attempts have been made in India to assess the practical importance of the ancient discoveries in the field of astrology, it

* Summary of a lecture delivered by the author at the All India Institute of Medical Sciences, New Delhi, on 25-2-1975.

is encouraging to find that some men of science-psychologists, doctors. etc., in the West have begun building up a new science of astral or stellar diagnosis on the demonstrable basis of facts and statistics. What is interesting is the fact that the investigations of these scientific workers have been indirectly corroborating many of the basic concepts of medical astrology as revealed by our ancient sages.

Throughout the centuries, astrology had had close connections with medicine. In ancient India, astrology and Ayurveda were intimately connected. An Ayurvedic doctor was required to be an astrologer too. But with the introduction of allopathy into India, the importance of astrology as a diagnostic test was reduced for a time. But now a reaction appears to have already set in largely due to the fact that a handful of leading medical men in Europe and America have been experimenting with medical astrology.

The dependency between the Sun and disease-incidence is indeed remarkable. Apart from wave-radiation, the Sun also sends off flows of corpuscles which are sometimes dabbed "the solar wind". Instruments installed on artificial satellites and rockets have shown that corpuscular radiation prevents flows of plasma which have magnetic fields of their own. This magnetic field interacts with the magnetic field of the earth and influences terrestrial phenomena. It can affect the electrical potential of an individual including the electrical activity of the brain. (The human brain, according to Vasiliev, radiates into surrounding space electro-magnetic energy in the form of radio-waves.) Due to this electric activity, various nerve impulses are sorted out and converted into sensations, thoughts and actions. It will be seen that it is the geometrical arrangements of planets that give rise to solar flares. In the astrological language, these planetary arrangements are the *yogas* which denote a definite pattern of events. Human beings, as Dr. Michael, M.R.C.S. says, have around them an energy-shell or field, which corresponds to the halo around a radio-active particle. The body radiates, the intensity varying with the different organs. Therefore its health or ill-health depends upon the harmony existing between its own radiation and the intensity of radiations received from the Sun, as well as from the cosmos at a given time.

In plain language, certain influences are exerted on our bodies by planets and stars and these are tendencies which can be dealt with by human beings in a positive or negative manner.

The experiments of Dr. Edson Andrews have

revealed that 82% of bleeding crises occur between the Moon's 1st and 3rd quarters. According to Prof. Revitz, there is considerable voltage increase in the electrical potential of a human being very 14 days at the time of New or Full Moon. These electrical changes correspond with sharp changes in the person's moods. Consequently the forces behind the Moon are said to aggravate maladjustments and conflicts.

The entire writing on *nishekavidhi* or conception deserves attention of modern gynaecologists. Clear ideas concerning the periodic fertility in a woman and their correlation to certain cosmic patterns have been given. According to gynaecologists Ogino and Knaus, the best fertile periods for conception in women (in the case of 28 and 30 days of menstrual cycles) are the 14th, 15th and 16th days from the commencement of menstruation. It appears that the pituitary controls the uterus up to the 16th day from the commencement of the menstruation, *i.e.*, the rupture of the graffian follicle. And according to the astrological work *Jataka Parijata*, the nights of 14, 15 and 16 are the best for conceiving offspring. These observations agree with the experimental evidence collected by Prof. Knaus that on the 15th night from the last day of menstruation, the ovum is born.

I should like to digress a bit and make a reference to the famous theory of "Thri-dosha". As commonly understood, Vata, Pitta and Sleshma are taken to mean gas, bile and phlegm respectively, and so the theory, in the face of it, may look somewhat unacceptable. But if we examine the concepts of Ayurveda in a critical way, we can find a close resemblance to western scientific thought.

The word *vata* is derived from the root *va*, meaning motion or indicative of motion ('वा' गतिगंधनयो रिति धातुः). The word *pitta* has its root in *tapa* (तपसं तयोपित्तं) meaning agitation, excitation, energy. *Kapha* or Sleshma means clasp, attraction, embrace, gravitation (श्लिषू आलिंगने) Chakrapani, the famous commentator, clarifies that one has to understand the inherent meaning of the three words vata, pitta and kapha as motivity, agility and gravity respectively. Put in a different way, these three qualities correspond to *motion*, *energy* and *inertia*. It may not be quite safe to assume that vata, pitta and kapha are just the three chemical substances of wind, bile and mucus.

It took years of theoretical reasoning and practical experimentation for science to accept that energy is a quality of matter till the presentation by Einstein of his theory of relativity. The discovery that any state of matter is formed by the three qualities of inertia (*sleshma*), energy (*pitta*) and motion (*vata*) should indeed go to Ayurveda.

As the great Susrutha says, just as the Sun, the Moon and Wind are necessary for the regular functioning of this world, so also it is *pitta, vata* and *sleshma* that regulate the health of the humun body. The effect of the three physical qualities (motion, energy and gravitation or inertia) on the living cell is on the same lines as it is in the cosmos.

The human ailments could be linked to the outcome of the gravitational pulls exerted by planets through rotation and revolution. The disequilibrium that arises in the *doshas* are due to the interaction between the field-forces emanating from the planets on the one side and the human organism on the other.

According to astrology, there are three groups of asterisms which are in line with the three *doshas* of Ayurveda. For instance, one born in a *vata* group of constellations would indeed be generally predisposed towards diseases arising from *vata*. Similarly, the planets and signs have also governance over the three *dhatus*. The Sun governs mostly *pitta* and a little of *vata*; the Moon mostly *vata*. etc. In the astrological literature, there is a thorough classification of diseases and the planetary patterns which cause them.

The Moon rules the mind, the Sun rules the soul

or self and Mercury rules the nervous system. Disorders arising from psychosis and neurosis and certain mental abnormalities—exaggeration of certain traits recognisable nearly in all people—are respectively caused by a combination of factors involving the Moon, Mercury, Mars, Saturn and the Nodes. Another psychologist, based on statistical research, has discovered a marked correspondence between different types of mental disorders and Mercury's afflictions. Obviously this reminds us of the age-old theory of the Hindus.

बुधचन्द्रौ केन्द्रगतौ नान्यग्रहसंयुतौ ।
न पतिवृष्ठौयोगोऽयंपैशाचस्तुऽतांत्पक्षोन्मदि ॥

meaning that if in a horoscope, the Moon and Mercury are in certain mutual dispositions afflicted by Mars, Saturn or the Nodes, it generally indicates mental disorders.

In actual practice, such a combination is present mostly in the horoscopes of persons suffering from obsessional neuroses, delusions and false beliefs. The declination or kranti of Mercury can give a clue as to whether a person's 'escape mechanism' will make him brood over the past, or hug the illusion of a fool's paradise in the present, or get into utopia of the future. But if there is a Jupiterian aspect, the picture is entirely changed. The person will be thoughtful, and will have a very understanding mind and good power of judgment. Remove the Moon and substitute Mars: you have the mechanical aptitude.

If one is suffering from mental fatigue, enhanced self-consciousness, development of an inferiority complex, general irritability, deep-seated fear, you can say that he has the Moon and Rahu in conjunction aspected by Saturn. If instead of the Moon, the affliction is centered on the Ascendant, the symptoms reveal themselves in the form of fatigue, eye tremour, nausea, soreness of the muscle, etc. Melancholia is produced by the simple conjunction of the Moon and Saturn. The person suffers from acute depression. Of course, constellational positions modify the effects. The Sun–Jupiter–Mars influences centered on Mercury or the Moon induce schizophrenia. If the ruling period happens to be that of Mars, he is prone to develop a persecution-complex. There are, of course, many forms of schizophrenia ranging from the day-dreamer and fantasy-weaver, down to the person who relapses into a katatonic condition. The essential pattern of the mental malady is clearly discernible in the horoscope. Studies in astro-psychology have revealed interesting details as regards the positive and negative traits of planets. On the positive side, the Moon is imaginative and variable. On the negative side irresponsible, moody and vacillating. Saturn is conscientious, clear headed, careful, self-controlled and conservatively conscious. On the negative side, he is narrow-minded, fixated, callous, miserly and ambitious in a selfish way.

On the positive side, Rahu is unconventional, independent and humanistic. On the negative side, he is unsocial, eccentric, neurotic and mildly destructive. The interpretation of these traits depends upon the experience and skill of the psycho-astrologer.

Many psychiatrists and psycho-analysts in the West have reported that they have found that horoscopes properly cast and intelligently interpreted is a valuable diagnostic test. The say that "a horoscope is more useful than a Rorschach test: A Rorschach shows only the patient's condition at the time the test is taken, whereas a horoscope reveals his basic psychological set-up".

The science of medical astrology deals with innumerable diseases. Diseases like consumption, blindness, hysteria, menstrual disorders, leprosy, rheumatism, gastric troubles, cardiac troubles, etc., have been dealt with extensively. Medical science with its improved instruments, X-ray, blood tests, cardiogram, etc., has no doubt made great strides towards better methods of diagnosis. But we have to note that medical knowledge should go beyond the science of the diseases. The physician must clearly distinguish the sick human being described in books from the concrete patient whom he has to treat. The physician's role is to discover the characteristics of the sick man's individuality, his resistance to pathogenic factors, his sensibility to pain, his past and his future. The outcome of an illness in a given individual has to be predicted not by a calculation of the probabilities but by a precise analysis of the organic, humoral and psychological personality of this individual. And it is only the horoscope that can provide this personality. By studying a horoscope, the physician will know the character of the patient whether his will is weak, and whether he is negative or emotional.

"Symptoms" give indications of disease which is in the process of materialising. But the horoscope can show the latent tendencies to diseases. When the planetary aspects have been stirred into action, the Dasa (period) and Bhukti (sub-period) dispositions give the diagnostician the key to it. The key to the mysteries of the human body lies shrouded in physiology. Medical science slices tissues, examines them under the microscope and seeks to find where The disease lies. The vital force which sustains life comes into the body from the fourth dimension. The reason why vitalism is neglected in modern scientific study is because there are no instruments capable of recording it directly whilst astrology provides a ready clue to the individualities of this force. "Electro-cardiographs, electro-encephalographs and measuring the metabolic rate are useful but cannot be revealing enough. There are not merely two main types of metabolism but in reality 12 different types, to which the only clue is astrology. Thus the Sun, when in Taurus and receiving the rays of Saturn, is tumour-forming and definitely points to the need for a special way of living which is quite different from an individual who has the Sun in Virgo and squared by Mars, for the latter does not proliferate the cells as does the former but breaks them down which readily ulcerate. Or when Saturn is in Aquarius and afflicts the Sun or the Moon, one is unaccountably nervous and jittery, has undue perspiration. Mars in Virgo, in bad aspect to the Sun and the Moon, gives hyper-insulism. They have the opposite of diabetes".

"There are also conditions not recognised in medicine which, none-the-less, markedly intefere with health. Those who have the Sun and the Moon in fiery signs or constellations are subject to a condition which, while not a disease, can have very detrimental results if not corrected. They tend to become dehydrated and if they live in a dry, warm, sunny climate will develop a nervous state almost impossible to diagnose." These are some of the important rules of an individual hygiene.

The extraordinary insight medical astrology affords the doctor into the nature of the whole of his patient has to be experienced to be believed. The quick insight he can obtain in differential diagnosis will save his time. For instance, Saturn in Libra, afflicting Mercury, induces very obscure spasms in the blood vessels of the kidney which frequently is only confirmed after many blood chemistry examinations simply because the condition comes and goes.

The position of the Sun is of the greatest consequence in understanding the vitality of a person. The causes of variation in solar radiation-intensities at the surface of the earth are the orbital distance between the Sun and the earth.

In July, when the Sun is in Cancer, for instance, the distance between the Sun and the earth is greatest. During this period, the biological energy waxes in the northern hemisphere and biological activity takes on a new pattern. In January (when the Sun is in Capricorn), he is nearest to the earth and the radiation-intensity exceeds by 7%. The horoscope is cast, taking the longitude and latitude of the place of birth, when the angular, solar and planetary positions affect animate or inanimate things.

Astrologically, one, who has Cancer rising, will have low vitality and he is too loath to follow the advice of others. He is suspicious by nature and lacks faith in others. But when the Sun is in this sign, the native has more vitality. Cancer has the rule over the stomach, diaphragm, upper lobes of the liver, the pancreas, and the gastric vein and serum of the blood. When the sign is afflicted, the person will be predisposed to indigestion, flatulence, dropsy and sclerosis—the exact disease depending upon the nature of afflicted planet. Cancer people are fond of food and are hearty eaters. Consequently, they are often afflicted with diseases which originate in wrong diet.

As a sample, I shall deal with one or two diseases. In the realms of appendicitis and heart diseases, thousands of horoscopes have been studied and the fundamental astrological ingredients of these diseases have been defined. Rahu and Mars, prominent in respect of the 6th house, reveal one's susceptibility to appendicitis and it will manifest under the directional influences of the afflicted planets. Because of this advance knowledge, one should adopt a plan of operation to counteract these influences.

Similarly with regard to heart diseases. As there are many forms of heart diseases, the indicators vary.

An affliction to the Sun is a *sine-qua-non* of heart trouble. When other planetary aspects enter this basic picture, further complications will appear. An affliction by Ketu reveals a heart weakened by poison from some malfunctioning organ or from another disease or infection. For coronary thrombosis, the affliction must take place in certain sensitive areas. While the physical and medical aspects of heart trouble are extremely involved and no two doctors like two astrologers completely agree in their diagnosis, the astrological influences are not difficult to trace. Closely allied with heart-difficulties in popular thinking is hyper-tension—high blood pleasure—supposed to be the most prevalent of all their ailments in America. In fact it has the distinction of being called "all American disease". While hyper-tension may occur without accompanying difficulties, it is most often associated with obesity, arteriosclerosis, gall-bladder troubles and kidney infections, though it may choose any malady as its partner in crime. The basic horoscopical indicators of hyper-tension are prominent angular Sun plus an afflicted Saturn or Mars. The planet from which the malefic (Saturn or Mars) draws its chief affliction (*e.g.*, square Mercury) will determine the nature of the accompanying difficulty, if there is to be one. An affliction from Jupiter predisposes to vascular construction by arterial deposits, from Rahu encourages high tension in daily life and will cause an increase in adrenal secretions. If the sign involved is Libra, it indicates accompanying kidney trouble caused by poisons from the upper alimentary tract. Similarly all other diseases can be judged fairly accurately.

The signs Aries to Pisces rule the different organs from head to foot and diseases of the organs concerned can be ascertained by studying the affliction.

A word about cancer. Though it is a frightening word, doctors say it is curable provided adequate treatment is begun in time. So the time factor is important. According to Dr. John J. Schifferes, cancer is said to be a group of diseases characterised by what he calls uncontrolled "lawless" growth of body cells. He also says that nobody yet knows what causes cancer. When American experts came out with their report, linking cigarette-smoking and cancer, many heavy puffers, it is said, stopped reading the report. The German experts say that polluted air is at the bottom of this disease. Now cancer is being linked with a good head of hair. After examining the hair patterns of 186 lung cancer patients in a hospital, two New Orlean physicians have come to the hair-raising conclusion that baldness and carcinoma do not go hand in hand. Lung cancer, they say, strikes three to four times as often in men with bountiful hair as in men with bald spots. This kind of hair-splitting logic can only lead to side-splitting laughter. A certain result of all this confusion is going to be that nobody will listen any more to experts, hair-brained or otherwise. But it opens up various other hilarious possibilities. More people in the West are getting taller, says a report; and more are also getting lung cancer; height and cancer are linked. People prone to bite their finger-nails or chew lead pencils or twist clips into surrealistic shapes are positively protected from cancer!

Whatever might be the opinion of experts, 200 or 300 horoscopes of cancer patients studied furnish material for certain broad conclusions. The constellation of Aslesha should be related to the Ascendant or the 6th house and afflicted by Mars.

Many of the readers may be familiar with astrological terminology. At least they will be knowing there are 12 signs of the zodiac, 27 stars and nine so-called planets. It is by a permutation and combination of the influences shed by these various bodies that an astrological materia-medica has been constructed. The fundamental purpose of medical astrology is to aid a physician in discovering what diseases would be produced under different planetary dispositions and the duration of such diseases When properly applied, astrology would quickly determine the seat of disease.

When medical astrology has so much to offer in the matter of disease diagnosis, why is it being ignored by the medical profession ? Conservatism and prejudice may be partly responsible and ignorance of the subject partly responsible.

Scientific orthodoxy could be as harmful as religious orthodoxy, but medical men who seem to be open-minded enough to make investigations which transcend the regions of accepted medical methods, are in the minority.

Research work would eventually tend to corroborate what ancient astrologers have written regarding the relationship existing between the motions of the heavenly bodied and man's health and sickness.

Science, by definition, should cover all fields of knowledge and if known laws of science cannot explain a set of phenomena, then the laws have to be suitably varied. It is interesting to note that while nothing is being done in India, in spite of the tall lalk of encouraging Ayurveda, the United States Department of Health, Education and Welfare has announced that there is enough evidence for expert research into health indications in a person's palm and finger prints. Dr. Rosner says that scientists have been aware for some time past that certain abnormal finger and palmar patterns occur in about 70% cases of mongolism.

The remedial aspect of astrology is also very important. For certains afflictions or *arishtayogas* in the horoscope, *i.e.*, inharmonious dispositions of planets which may express themselves as mental or physical afflictions, remedial measures based on *mantrasastra* are suggested in ancient texts.

The *arishtayogas* merely indicate the deficiency of the requisite or normal energy-quanta and this can be compensated by *mantras* which are nothing but packets or bundles of adjusted forms of sound vibrations. Recent researches carried on sound-waves have clearly shown their therapeutical value. In prescribing different types of mantras for different types of mental and physical afflictions, our ancient medical men like Dhanvantri, Susruta, etc., seem to have been alive to the tremendous potentiality of sound vibrations.

XII

*ASTROLOGY Vs FUTUROLOGY

The so-called Futurology is the latest addition to the list of modern sciences or speculations about how human affairs look like in the distant future—2000 A.D., 4000 A.D., etc., etc. Recently hundreds of "scientists, teachers, sociologists", etc., met in America to "visualise the meaning of the 21st century". They claim that "futurology" has now been accorded (perhaps by themselves) "the status of an important discipline, not only because it represents an essential function of the thinking man but also because it brings within its ambit all human knowledge and all sciences and arts and strives to integrate them". And what is astrology but futurology built on sounder and more systematic mathematical laws. But the scientist would rather coin a new term and base his findings on speculations than to admit astrology into the comity of so-called accepted

* Summary of a lecture delivered by the Author at the Indian Institute of World Culture, Bangalore, on 1st January 1976.

sciences. Many a scientist have made up minds and refuse to concede that before they knew anything of futurology, there were savants and sages in this part of the world who had made deep studies of laws of nature which linked happenings on the earth with happenings in the cosmos.

Even in the West, there are some fair-minded scientists who admit that at all the boundaries of science, they come up against what are perhaps the "inherent limitations of human understanding".

Take, for example, the chasm that exists between what biology describes and what the mind experiences. If we try to contemplate the limits of space or the beginning of time, we encounter insoluble contradictions in physical sciences. Why should numerical and geometrical laws govern the transformations of the "transient entities of the atomic and sub-atomic world"? The triumph of structural chemistry is said to be an essential understanding of the genetic code in living matter. But why the code-bearing molecules can replicate themselves only in a living cell and not in isolation is baffling the scientists.

The confusion evident in the thinking of the present-day scientists about the universe, life and matter and future of mankind is clearly reflected in the often contradictory statements made by different eminent scientists on the same subject.

The ancient Hindu savants declared that gravitation (गुरुत्वाकर्षण) was a property (स्वभाव) of matter and Newton said the same thing. The German philosopher Ernest Mach said that local behaviour of matter is influenced by the distant parts of the universe —an idea which appears to have been borrowed by Dr. Hoyle, but which indeed is the basic assumption of astrological science.

There is a flood of new theories let loose by some of the "futurologists" who, wearing the mantle of modern science, indulge in statements which smack of scare-mongering and amusement.

The latest bogey of these scientists is that the world is faced with the grim prospect of population-explosion. These scare-mongers are definite that the "next 75 years will be a most critical period in man's history. We will face disaster".

According to Sir Julian Huxley population increase is the "key-problem of our age". According to Peter Bishop, "there is right with us today a growing peril more appalling even than a H-Bomb explosion". The British astronomer Hoyle widens his horizon and forecasts that in 5000 A.D. a new species will inhabit the earth. He is "precise", unlike astrologers who indulge in probability, that in the year 2000 A.D., the world population will be 6,000 million ; in 2250 A.D., it will be 25,000 million ; and in 2400 A.D.—only 428 years away from now—man will have only standing room on this planet. How can we allow such an uncontrolled growth ? Prof. Hoyle opines that this can be stopped not merely by cutting the birth-rate but by "raising the death-rate". Explode a couple of hydrogen bombs now and the world will be safer by 2400 A.D. The scientists do not stop at that. They go further and say that "there will be a collapse of the world's population after it has touched a peak of 25,000 million ; and please mark the succeeding statement—in 300 years' time (from the time of peak-point), there will be population collapse to the level of 2000 million. And this will again rise to the peak, collapse, rise, collapse, etc.—constantly oscillating ; and following a "process of biological distillation" man will be quite another creature by the end of 6999 A.D. All this is very exciting coming as it does from scientists—futurologists and not from astrologers.

Then we have the bleak forecast of the human race automatically annihilating itself on Friday 13-11-2026. This is the conclusion of the brain-child of the scientist—a computer. This was programmed some time ago at the National Institute of Natural Resources in Mexico City by feeding "birth-rate, mortality trends, existing food resources and furure forecasts". According to the forecast of this computer, "our great-grandchildren will be the last men and women to walk on the earth as we know it".

If, according to Hoyle, the world population will be 6,000 million in 2000 A.D. the Mexico scientists estimate the population to be 7,000 millions. Between the calculation of two modern scientists, the difference is just 1,000 million!—not 100, 1,000s or even 1 million. Yet they are scientists and no scientist dare criticise them because their conclusions are based on "scientific" faces.

And we have the strange phenomenon of some "scientists" in India who perhaps ignorant of the latest findings in physical sciences establishing correlations between planetary movements and terrestrial events cry day in and day out that astrology is no science because no one predicted the date of this or that event. Stretching the argument of these "scientists", the inference is evident because 'Aryabhata' was a nuisance, 'Bhaskara' a flop, and Sri Harikota launching a miserable failure, space-science is no science !

We can fully sympathise with the plight of such "scientists" who have made up or closed minds and who consider it their privilege to attack astrology day in and day out not on intellectual or logical levels but on loose and ignorant generalisations.

Most of these experts like Professor Barry Commoner and Dr. Heiuz Von Porster of the burgeoise West or Mr. Igor Vernadski of Socialist Russia predict world-destruction through over-population or some gigantic upheaval in space or "we will poison ourselves to death" even during the next century.

There are other scientists, absolute pessimists, like Jacques Piccard who thinks that he "was seriously doubtful whether mankind would last out another hundred years." According to others yet, the world will end "around the year 2070" because of "atomic threat and widespread suicidal pollution".

These prophets of doom, all scientists enjoying the patronage of civilised Governments all over the world and not poor astrologers who have to depend upon their own resources and what little patronage they get from the thinking public, do not leave us here. They go further and assert categorically that "unless the birth-rate is drastically checked"—here we have a silver lining—"civilisation as we know it is doomed. Governments will collapse, law and order will vanish, mass-rioting, plagues and disease will sweep the earth". Waht is appalling is, mankind will literally go back to the jungle! To these futurologists of this way of thinking, the population-explosion and all the hell it will let loose on us are grim possibilities of fact "in the foreseeable future". If we are to believe these speculators, then by the time you complete reading this chapter "another 1,800 babies will have uttered their first cry" Even in regard to the time-factor as to when this catastrophe will befall the earth, they are not uncertain though not quite definite. Just 45 years from now and you are doomed!

The scare-mongering of futurologists is not confined merely to the doom of our planet by population-explosion. Other catastrophes are also anticipated.

According to Dr. Bruce C. Heazen of the La Mount Geological Observatory, the earth's magnetic field will reverse in about 4000 A.D. What is the consequence? The earth's magnetic field blinks and all life on earth including of course that of the puiny creature Man will be unprotected from bombardment from cosmic rays and the umbrella in space now protecting you, me and Dr. Bruce is removed. Drastic mutations in living things will be caused by cosmic rays and the consequences of this "mutation epidemic" cannot be grasped. Dr. Heazen also tells us that this "magnetic switch" has occurred before in the history of the earth and that it happens *every 700,000 to a million* (italics ours) years.

The first signs of the mutation epidemic would be "trouble with compasses". Scientists will hold public debates—if of course their thinking power is not affected by the cosmic forces bombarding them when there is no more the earth's magnetic field to shield them of how to meet the coming catastrophe.

"Biologists would soon announce that planets and animals were producing new species. The spigot of evolution would be turned on. New flowers, new insects would emerge. Perhaps new virus and bacteria that would ignore all of man's antibiotics would cause a rise in the death-rate.

"Then the full blow would fall when it was found that more and more babies were being born freaks. The thalidomide episode in Europe would be nothing to the generation of monsters being born all over the world.

"With the technological progress that one might imagine in the next 2,000 years, could man create his own umbrella of magnetism, possibly with the energy of fusion reactions ?

"Or would it help to send prospective parents into deep caves beyond the reach of cosmic radiation ?

"Since the death-rate was rising and many of

the children born could not survive, there would be a decrease in the earth's human population. Controls on population which must certainly be put into effect on this crowded planet long before the year 4000, might have to be removed in order to keep the species going at all." And in the year of grace 4001 A.D. there would be the birth of the first child of the new super-human race !

The readings of futurologists given above are indeed dark and pessimistic. Of course brighter shades contradicting the evil indications are also not missing.

According to Henry Dreyfus, by 2000 A.D., "moderately well-off people will have homes filled with marvels of invention". If you happen to be "moderately well-off" and are lucky enough to live for another 20 years, you will be able to "vary the lighting in your house" to match your mood and cool crisp lighting for reading or warm pink lighting for dining. Your wife will bake a cake in a "micro-wave oven" which cooks food without heating the oven and when the meal is over "the disposal plastic-plates and cutlery will be ground to dust and automatically flushed away". Other prophecies are : "Whole families will be able to visit each other by T.V. The cheapest ordinary car will be a turbo-propelled machine doing 150 miles an hour suspended one foot above the ground on an air cushion".

According to Dr. Joseph Schultz, "women in 2000 A.D. will have purple or orange hair and pale blue or orange skin make-up. They can sleep with their make-up in tact".

Then there are celestial catastrophes anticipated by astronomers of the Sun burning out, or an extra-terrestrial object smashing the earth or putting the solar system out of gear. The chances of the Sun exploding "once during its life-time", say the astronomers, "are quite high". If and when the explosion does occur, how will be the scene on the earth just eight minutes after ? Fearful beyond description ?

"The sky will be filled with weird patterns of white hot fire. All organic matter, all life, will be burnt to a cinder, the seas will boil away. As the air on the side of the earth facing the Sun goes up with heat, cold air will rush in from the night side at frightful speeds destroying everything in its path. Where it will be night, life will be asphyxiated. The dead matter will turn into ash when exposed to the Sun.

"A few days later, burning gases from the Sun will envolop the dead earth which, getting hotter and hotter, will melt, turn into gas and steal way into the dead night of space in the form of the primordial particles from which it took the shape we know." It is not clear what the Professor means by "a few days later"—as there can be no day anywhere in the solar system when the Sun is dead. But that is of course scientific reasoning which cannot be questioned.

The speculations of many of these scientists are of course supported by a series of calculations and "statistical studies" which have all the glitter of scientific reasoning about them but which are based on assumptions which have themselves to be definitely proved.

The ancient Maharshis have clearly shown that crop failures, financial slumps, wars, earthquakes and birth and death rates are all correlated to solar radiation. In other words, the usual principles of astrology can explain the present population crisis as they can explain every other crisis and conflict which twentieth-century mankind is said to face. Apart from contraception, economic circumstances, abortion, étc., the important factors contributing to differential fertility, is the presence or absence of the Beeja and Kshetra factors in the horoscopes of different persons. These again depend upon the moment of birth, that is the planetary juxtapositions. While scientists may be justified in anticipating a fearful future for the world by population increase, basing their conclusions on their own pet theories, we, as students of astrology, are constrained to feel that there is no astrological basis for the fear that "human reproduction will outrun resources".

There is also a recognisable connection between the movements of the equinox and long-range terrestrial affairs such as population trends, historical changes, mass movements, etc. At the moment, the equinox is in 7° 57′ Pisces in the second quarter of Uttarabhadra ruled by Saturn but the Navamsa being Virgo. The equinox entered the Nadi Amsa of *maitri* in 1956. It passes through *mandira* (1974) and *varuna* (1984) gettig into *jalaplava* in 1998. This will be just about the time of anticipated population-explosion. When it enters *madira*, the world is in for a lot of carnage by wars, pestilences and plagues. The equinoxial movement in *jalaplava* (Navamsa of Mercury ruling the nervous system, etc). produces immense stress on human beings. Stress makes for enlarged adrenals and adrenal glands have been cited as a population safety-valve. Thus there is absolutely no indication of the earth facing the calamity the scientists think it does. By A.D. 2000, when Jupiter and Saturn will again be conjoined in Aries, the world's equilibrium will have been considerably restored by the outbreaks of wars, earthquakes, famine, etc., and the falling down of birth-rates.

Whatever may be the forecasts of futurologists, cosmologists and prophets of doom, a reference to Hindu astronomical literature can give us a clue based on astronomical factors as to when the world or the existing order of things is likely to come to an end. Not until this period comes is there any prospect of the catastrophes envisaged by modern "scientific" futurologists ever happening.

The theory of Yugas has a scientific basis and is not merely based upon fantastic imaginativeness and arbitrary theorisings, as some modern savants want us to believe. The "Sankalpa", which every Hindu is expected to know and which is recited at every ceremony, is the key to unfold the whole mystery that enshrouds the view of the time at which the earth assumed its present form. The Hindu astronomers, assuming that the planets were in a line of mean conjunction with the first point of Aries at the beginning of a Mahayuga and that these planets will occupy the same positions at the beginning of the next Mahayuga, at a place on equator, whose longitude is 76° E. of Greenwich calculated the period of a Mahayuga at 4,320,000 years which they supposed to be the L.C.M. of the different number of days taken by each planet to make one revolution round the zodiac. As most readers must be aware, a Mahayuga or Chaturyuga is made up of Krita, Treta, Dwapara and Kali and contains 12,000 Deva or 4,320,000 ordinary years. 71 Mahayugas constitute one Manvantra (308,448,000 years) and 14 Manvantaras or Manus make up one Kalpa or Brahmadina or Brahma's day (4,320,000,000 years).

Now according to the Sankalpa, already six Manvantaras have passed in the present Kalpa and the seventh is now going on. There are still seven more Manvataras to come.

In the 7th Manvantara, 27 Mahayugas have passed and we are now in the last Yuga of the 28th Mahayuga. We can, therefore, compute the number of years passed in the present Kalpa thus :

Dawn of the Kalpa		1,728,000 years
6 Manus or Manvantaras		1,850,688,000 years
Twenty-seven Mahayugas....		116,640,000 years
In the 28th Mahayuga :		
Krita	1,728,000	
Treta	1,296,000	
Dwapara	864,000	
Kali	5,080	3,893,080 years
		1,972,949,080 years
Deduct time occupied in creation		17,064,000 years
Total from the end of present creation		1,955,885,080 years

We are still in the beginning of Kaliyuga and have yet to pass 426,920 years before the present Yuga ends. Therefore, there is no prospect of a deluge or the annihilation of the earth in our lifetime or in that of even our great-great-grandchildren. Hindu astronomers have assigned 315 trillion mortal years as Brahma's age or the life-span of the universe.

There are two major Pralayas or dissolutions: *Naimittika* or incidental destruction of all creation, of all the lives that have a form, but not of the substance. The substance remains in *status quo* till the new dawn in that Brahmaratri. The universe is thus alternately created from and dissolved into its material cause at the end of every Brahmaratri and Brahmadina. The second is *Prakritika* or Mahapralaya—the great Dissolution which is said to occur at the end of the life-period of Brahma. In this final Pralaya, everything in the universe, material as well as non-material, is dissolved into atoms.

The creative scientist is usually more concerned with the relation of things to one another than with mere analysis of what these things are. And a real astrologer is not different. His quest is for the questions which still remain the most absorbing and the oldest of all: the cosmos and its relation to mankind.

APPENDIX

Prof. Carl Jung's letter to Prof. B. V. Raman

Kusnacht–Zch., September 6th 1947

DEAR PROF. RAMAN,

I haven't, yet received THE ASTROLOGICAL MAGAZINE, but I will answer your letter nevertheless.

Since you want to know my opinion about astrology I can tell you that I've been interested in this particular activity of the human mind since more than 30 years. As I am a psychologist, I am chiefly interested in the particular light the horoscope sheds on certain complications in the character. In cases of difficult psychological diagnosis I usually get a horoscope in order to have a further point of view from an entirely different angle. *I must say that I very often found that the astrological data elucidated certain points which I otherwise would have been unable to understand.* From such experiences I formed the opinion that astrology is of particular interest to the psychologist, since it contains a sort of psychological experience which we call "projected"—this means that we find the psychological facts as it were in the constellations. This originally gave rise to the idea that these factors derive from the stars, whereas they are merely in a relation of synchronicity with them. I admit that this is a very curious fact which throws a peculiar light on the structure of the human mind.

What I miss in astrological literature is chiefly the statistical method by which certain fundamental facts could be scientifically established.

Hoping that this answer meets your request.

I remain,
Yours sincerely,
(Sd.) C. G. JUNG.

REFERENCES CONSULTED

An Introduction to the Study of Astrology *by B. Suryanarain Rao*

Human Knowledge, Its Scope and Limits *by Bertrand Russel*

Secret of the Golden Flower *by Carl Jung*

Epidemic Catastrophes and the Period Activity of the Sun *by Tchijevsky*

Contributions to Analytical Psychology *by Carl Jung*

A Study in History *by A. J. Toynbee*

Astrology's Place in the World of Science *by Arnold W. Meyer*

Mainsprings of Civilisation *by Ellsworth Huntington*

Actions of Radiations on Living Cells *by W. E. Lea*

The Secret of Life *by Georges Lakhovsky*

A Text-Book of Astrology *by A. J. Pearce*

Astrology in Everyday Life *by Rupert Gleadow*

Marxism, Materialism, Determinism and Dialectics *by D. N. Das Gupta*

Brahma Sutras of Vyasa (English Translation) *by Sridhar Majumdar*

New Background of Science *by James Jeans*

The Universe in the Light of Modern Physics *by Planc*

The Universe Around Us *by James Jeans*

Astrology of Personality *by Dane Rudhyar*

A Brief History of Astrology *by Temple Hungad*

Hindu Astrology *by Mankari Pande*

Astrology, Destiny and Cosmic Factors *by V. Gore*

D'Astro-Biologie *by K. E. Krafft*
Der Geist der Astrologie *by George Muller*
Plato's Cosmology *Translated by F. M. Cornford*
The Metaphysical Foundations of Modern Science
by Edwin A. Burth
Reach of the Mind *by J. B. Rhine*
The Psychology of Time *by Mary Stuart*
Yoga Vasista
Brihadaranyaka Upanishad (English Translation)
by Swami Madhavananda
Ethical Relativity *by E. A. Westermarek*
The Invisible Influence *by Alexander Canon*
American Astrology—1942, 1944 and 1945
Economic Journal—1921
Journal of the Royal Statistical Society—1922
Arthasastra of Kautilya (English Translation)
by R. Shama Shastry
Brihat Jataka
Brihat Parasara Hora
Panchasiddanthika
Brihat Samhita
Muhurtha Chintamani
Agni Purana
Yoga Sutras of Patanjali
Gheran Samhita